A TALE OF TWO FOOTBALL TOWNS & MILLWALL F.C.

My dad's story by Joe Broadfoot

First published in 2012

by Londinium Publishing Limited

13 Hereford Gardens, London SE13 5LU

All rights reserved

Copyright © Joe Broadfoot, 2012

The right of Joe Broadfoot to be identified as the author of this work has been asserted in accordance with Section 77 of the Copyright, Designs and Patents Act 1988

ISBN-13:
978-1480208469

ISBN-10:
1480208469

ACKNOWLEDGMENTS

I would like to thank the following people for their help and support: Theo Foley, Frank Grande, Ian Davies, my friends and all the family, particularly my mum, Jean. Of course, most of all I have to thank my dad, Joe Broadfoot Senior, for agreeing to tell me his life story.

CONTENTS

Chapter 1	6
Chapter 2	11
Chapter 3	15
Chapter 4	19
Chapter 5	22
Chapter 6	25
Chapter 7	28
Chapter 8	31
Chapter 9	34
Chapter 10	37
Chapter 11	39
Chapter 12	42
Chapter 13	45
Chapter 14	47
Chapter 15	51
Chapter 16	55
Chapter 17	61
Chapter 18	67
Chapter 19	83
Chapter 20	91

JOE BROADFOOT

Career Stats   100

Brief biography   103

About the author   104

Chapter 1: I want you to remember, I'm 71-years-old. A lot of what I'm going to tell you happened over 50 years ago, yet I'd like to get it right, so I'm not going to rush it. I'm going to tell it in my own time.

It'll be what I consider to be "the truth". That's not always the case when people talk or write about the past. Let's just say when I hear other people's accounts about what happened to me in the past, I have to say I don't remember the same events in the same way at all. I'm not trying to make my story sound better than it really was and I'm not trying to exaggerate. I'm just telling you my story the way I remember it.

It all started with me scoring goals at Roan Grammar School, near Blackheath, London. It got mentioned in the school magazine: 'Twenty-nine goals in twelve games'. Not bad for a tiny little 14-year-old, who lost his mother in his first term at secondary school. That loss didn't make life any easier on the academic front at a "clever" school, but I could just go out and play football when I wanted.

My auntie, who came to my house to look after me, couldn't stop me going out playing cricket or football. I just loved getting out and about. I was an outdoors person. I lived next door to Mountsfield Park, so I'd just hop over the fence and I was in the park, where I was in my element.

Anyway, it all started happening for me in a professional sense when I left school. I was asked to leave school because one: I was caught riding my bike in Greenwich Park and two:

A TALE OF TWO FOOTBALL TOWNS & MILLWALL F.C.

I'd been shouting out the classroom window to one of the masters of Vanbrugh Park, the school adjacent to mine. My mates had spotted this teacher, so I shouted something at him, as you do. Well, he didn't like it much so he came into our school to report it to the headmaster, Mr Gilbert. Our head's deputy, Mr Berry, wanted to cane me, but Mr Gilbert said to me: "You might as well leave. You're leaving at Christmas anyway. There's only 3 weeks to go and you're becoming a nuisance." I took his hint and I was gone.

I went to work for my dad, who had a light engineering firm. He was a blacksmith by trade. He had his own company and I started at there at the age of 15 and a half. I was now in a man's world.

I stopped playing football for a while. But one day, I played for the firm I was working for and scored a hat-trick on Blackheath and they put me in their first team. Funnily enough, given I went on to play for The Lions, the team was called Lion Athletic. They put me on the wing. It was the same with my cousin's team. My cousin got me playing on a Sunday morning for a team called Mottingham South.

I'm not sure why I didn't play more as a striker as I once scored 10 goals in a game, playing for the Boys' Brigade at Ladywell Recreation Ground. One was a header from a corner. I was quite pleased about that as I rarely scored with my head. Not surprising, as I was about five-foot nothing! Anyway, I played for that team up until the age of 15. We were in the second division of our league and I think we were called the 61st Boys' Brigade Company.

I used to enjoy playing cricket in the summer, as well. So I was an all-round sportsman. I didn't have the money to play proper tennis, but we used to make our own tennis rackets with bats and play in the road outside my house. There was no traffic in those days, so it was reasonably safe. As well as that, I used to run. I remember winning a sprinting prize, when I was about five. It was just after World War Two. I came in second place in some race for the Queen's Coronation in June 1953. I let my brother win that one and everyone was pleased about that.

So you could say I was a pretty fit kid. What made my sporting life better was going to a secondary school like the Roan. I was lucky enough to go to the only grammar school in south-east London that specialised in football.

Roan was making a habit of producing good footballers. Not long before I left that school, Brian Kinsey joined Charlton. Me and Brian share the same birthday, but he's two years older than me. He went on to play around 400 games for Charlton Athletic. As a professional, I even played against him, as he was a left back and I was a right winger. I was playing for Ipswich Town, at the time, and I think Brian got the better of me. I certainly don't remember having a very good game, but we still managed a 1-1 draw.

Decades later, there were other Old Roans who cracked it in the football sense. Gary Micklewhite got signed by Manchester United, but moved onto Queens Park Rangers without playing a game at United. It was a good move back to London for him, as he got to play in the 1982 FA Cup final.

A TALE OF TWO FOOTBALL TOWNS & MILLWALL F.C.

QPR lost after a replay and Gary ended up moving to Derby County, before ending his professional career at Gillingham. Then there was Phil Coleman, who played for Millwall and David Campbell, who signed for Charlton. That was in the days when Roan was a grammar school. When it went comprehensive, players like David Hillier, who played for Arsenal and Portsmouth, still came through, but Old Roans didn't talk about them so much as it was usually only the ex-grammar school kids that ended up frequenting the Old Roan club in Kidbrooke Park Road. That club's celebrating its 100th anniversary and it's a place where I've enjoyed a lot of precious sporting memories. Playing cricket, I scored fifty runs, one hundred times there, so you could call it my 'happy place'. I played against former international cricketers like Derek Underwood.

I would have loved to have played professional cricket, but football took a lot out of you. Of course, the Compton brothers, Leslie and Denis, managed to have careers in both sports, but they were both before my time, in a professional sense. However, I was lucky enough to watch Denis Compton playing on the left wing for Arsenal against Charlton. There's some old news reel footage on the Internet nowadays of Denis scoring in Arsenal's 7-1 demolition of the Addicks back in 1943 at Wembley in a cup final. Well, I used to go to the Valley a lot to see the best footballers in action and I'll never forget seeing Denis Compton's cracking left-foot volley. But Denis ended up having knee trouble, a bit like I suffered from. Like me, he had surgery, and I'm told Denis's knee cap is now in a biscuit tin at Lord's Cricket Ground. It makes me wonder where my removed cartilages will end up!

A TALE OF TWO FOOTBALL TOWNS & MILLWALL F.C.

Chapter 2: As I was saying in the last chapter, just before I joined Millwall, I was playing for Lion Athletic, which would you believe it was a pub team? The Lion pub's not there anymore, but it was located on the junction opposite where McDonald's is in Surrey Quays, which we knew as Surrey Docks. The guy who ran that team knew the groundsman at Millwall. I was only about 5 foot one or two, by then, but I knew he'd been telling everyone about this little fella he had playing on the wing. And naturally, he'd also been telling the groundsman that I was talented and deserved a trial at Millwall.

So I got my chance. I went down to Millwall for the last juniors' game in the South East London Counties League in 1957. I started on the left wing, but I got told to move over to the right wing for the second half. We were losing 1-0 to Queens Park Rangers and then with 10 minutes to go, I came into the middle and I managed to score a goal.

Afterwards, they said: "Well done, we'll be in contact." They did contact me, around about July. Millwall asked me to come down and talk to them, which I did. I signed as an amateur and then I started training twice a week, which made a hell of a difference to my game. We did a lot of running without the ball, so my fitness was improving all the time. The professionals trained five times a week, so their fitness levels were even higher. Back then, it was fitness that was the main difference between amateurs and professionals.

Talking about the difference between amateurs and professionals for a moment, I made a little joke once, after my playing days were over, at the expense of former Millwall utility player, Lucas Neill. Everyone watching the Lions at the time could see Lucas was destined for greater things and when I saw him after one pre-season game at Newport

County AFC in the club's bar. There he was sitting down, drinking juice, munching crisps and looking proud because he'd just represented his beloved Australia in the Olympics.

"Oi, Lucas," I shouted to him. "You just got back from the Olympics?"

"Yeah, that's right."

"Olympics? That's for amateurs, ain't it?"

He didn't reply, but he looked pretty cheesed off. He was a nice guy, though, Lucas. I remember watching him training at Millwall, and he was so intense. Maybe too intense, as he used to go mad at himself, effing and blinding if he made a mistake. Anyway, he must have been doing something right to make such a great career for himself.

I remember buying Lucas a pint in the player's lounge at the Den, after he scored his first goal for Millwall, back in the 1990s.

"Well done, Lucas," I said. "One goal, only 66 more to score to beat my record. I'll get you another pint when you do."

Anyway, I knew I was a dead cert to win that bet! Poor old Lucas used to get played in so many different positions, mostly defensive, so there was no chance of him banging in loads of goals. Nevertheless, he was a class act and sorely missed when he got sold, much too cheaply in my opinion by the erstwhile chairman Theo Paphitis to Blackburn Rovers. If the figures are correct, £600k upfront followed by additional £400k based upon appearances was not market value for a player of Lucas' quality.

A TALE OF TWO FOOTBALL TOWNS & MILLWALL F.C.

That digression was a bit longer than I intended. Apologies for that!

So, as I was saying, amateurs were a long way behind professionals in the late 1950s in terms of their fitness levels, but not necessarily in regard to skill.

But although I was an amateur at Millwall now, things were going pretty well for me. I was scoring a few goals for the juniors, playing on the right wing. We beat Portsmouth 7-1 and we beat West Ham 6-1. We even beat Chelsea 2-1, but they obviously didn't have all their best players, like Jimmy Greaves and Barry Bridges, playing. Nonetheless, Chelsea fielded a good side against us. David Cliss, who made the Blues' first-team was in that juniors team, and some other big names to be. The fact that Chelsea made it to the Youth Cup final in 1957-58 shows how good they were, so for us to beat them was a decent achievement. Especially as we beat them on their ground! So we weren't that bad a team ourselves!

By the end of September or start of October, Millwall were playing a friendly against an Isthmian League XI and they asked me to play on the right wing. I couldn't believe it. So I went down there with my teddy boy haircut and my old football boots. We won about 5-1. My crowning glory in that game was taking a corner that John Shepherd headed in. He ran across to congratulate me and made me feel like I'd done something wonderful.

Nevertheless, I didn't really think I'd be signed on professional terms. I didn't really think about it at all. I only used to think about what we were going to do next. 'One game at a time,' as they often say in football!

Except, I wouldn't always be thinking about football. I'd be thinking: 'Where will I go out tonight?' I never worried about making a career from the game.

After all, I was doing a job that I enjoyed. I'd packed up my job with my dad. That was too much like hard work! I was getting my hands dirty and it was too cold being an apprentice blacksmith, so instead I worked on a bag wash in Bermondsey. I enjoyed that because it was energetic and you moved around a lot. The hours were 7 until 7 on a Monday but gradually it tailed away so by Friday you were in about 10 or half past 10 and finished by about 1. I used to get a few quid in tips, as well. I was up and down the flats all around the area where Millwall's new ground is now so, in a sense, it was good training for me in more ways than one!

As well as that, I was training away at Millwall and I'd scored about half a dozen goals from the right wing and all was going well apart from a slight injury I'd sustained to my right angle. It was nothing major, though, so I suppose you could say I was continuing to make steady progress.

Something big was about to happen to me, around the time of the Munich air disaster (6th February 1958) that cruelly struck down so many "Busby Babes" in their prime.

I'll let you know more about that in the next chapter.

A TALE OF TWO FOOTBALL TOWNS & MILLWALL F.C.

Chapter 3: About two weeks before my 18th birthday (4th March 1958), Millwall asked me to sign professional. As a signing-on fee, I got between £10 and £20, I can't remember exactly.

But I do know what I signed on for: it was six pounds a week during the football season, plus four pounds a week in the summer. If I got in the first team, I got an extra fiver a week and if I was playing for the reserves, I think I got a quid extra. Bonuses then were two pounds for a win and one for a draw.

It wasn't the money that appealed to me. I was going to say it was "love of the game", but "love" is a strong word. I'd say I did it simply because I wanted to. It was a lot better than working in a factory or running up and down stairs doing the bag wash, as I had been for a while.

So I was very happy to sign "pro". To celebrate, I bought a new coat with my signing-on fee.

I immediately started featuring for the reserves on a regular basis, playing against good teams like Spurs and Chelsea. We used to lose by a single goal usually, so I didn't think I was doing that well. Somehow, I used to get through these games, almost just going through the motions. My view, at the time, was: "this is good fun". I never felt then, like some young footballers do, that I was destined to be a great player. I was simply doing what I really enjoyed.

I had a relaxing summer in 1958, living on my four pounds a week, listening to pop songs on my record player like 'Volare' by Dean Martin, which was later changed to "Oh Wisey!" by the Millwall fans during the Dennis Wise era.

My dad was to break my leisurely mood. "Son," he said, in his thick Glaswegian accent – he was from the notorious Gorbals my dad – "you'd better get in the first-team this year, or Millwall will kick you out." I just wanted to lay back and listen to the Coasters singing 'Yakety Yak'. It had never really occurred to me that my footballing career could be over before it had really started. It was a bit of a wake-up call. For a moment, at least.

Then I thought about it. I wasn't completely resting on my laurels. I was still doing a bit of canvassing for the bag wash company, who'd helped get me this far in football through their connections.

I couldn't get away from the bottom line which was this: I was a bit of a tearaway. My mum wasn't around to keep an eye on me, so that probably didn't help.

Basically, I never really thought ahead. So despite my dad's words, I just carried on doing what I was doing.

The season started. For me, it was still reserve-team football. We went to Southampton. I think it ended 0-0. We didn't lose anyway. But the Saints were, at the time, doing better than Millwall. They'd finished 6th in the Third Division South in the previous season whereas we'd ended up 23rd!

I remember it was a warm day. I felt quite happy. I'd trained hard over the summer. I was young and fit. Johnny Short, our

A TALE OF TWO FOOTBALL TOWNS & MILLWALL F.C.

trainer, used to make us run alright! We used to run to Greenwich Park from Bermondsey, so it was a fair old distance. To make it more grueling, it was up and down hills.

So I felt well prepared for this game against Southampton's reserves. Nevertheless, I don't really feel I gave their defence much to worry about on that day.

My view was I'd done better at the tail end of the season before. I think I did better in a game for the reserves at Portsmouth where we lost 6-1. Pompey were in the top flight and had a good team with the likes of Ray Crawford and Derek Dougan playing upfront. In that game, I remember their left back steaming into me. It was a wet day, so he slid in and my knees caught him in the goolies. He ended up getting carried off.

I also remember playing quite well in another heavy defeat, this time at top-flight Birmingham. We had three or four amateurs in our reserve team, whereas the Blues had an exciting right winger, Mike Hellawell, who ended up playing for England.

You tend to remember wingers, as you've only got to run past your marker two or three times and everyone starts going: 'Who's that, who's that?' It's nearly as good as scoring goals.

Anyway, I digress. Let's go back to me playing away at Southampton for the reserves. The first team had played Gillingham on the opening day of the season and had won 2-1, so they'd got off to a good start. Then they went to Walsall, on the Monday night, and lost 2-1.

It was a reasonable start to the season. Two points from two games. So imagine my surprise, on Friday, when I saw the team sheet for the next game pinned up on the wall. There it was. My name was on it!

I'll let you know about what happened next in the following chapter.

A TALE OF TWO FOOTBALL TOWNS & MILLWALL F.C.

Chapter 4: Mmm. Where was I? Let's see. I was talking about the Millwall first team playing Gillingham on the opening day of the season and winning 2-1, but going to Walsall, on the Monday night, and losing 2-1.

Not the worst start to a season of all time, especially in the days of 2 points for a win! So imagine my surprise, when on four days later, I saw my name on the team sheet for the next game pinned up on the wall.

It was Friday afternoon and I was absolutely gobsmacked. I couldn't sleep that night, as you'd expect. Not the best preparation for a match!

I couldn't calm down at all when Saturday afternoon finally came around. I was a lively little lad at the best of times, and for my first Millwall game, I got changed first before the rest of the team and there I was chatting away non-stop waiting for the kick off.

But about five minutes before we were due to go out, someone put his head through the dressing door and said: 'Carlisle United haven't arrived yet!' A few minutes later, the same voice told us the opposition had arrived and were getting changed on the coach, which was a relief to me, as you can imagine!

Anyway, we kicked off a little bit late. I don't know if Carlisle got in trouble or not with the football authorities, but the Old Kent Road was notorious for traffic congestion so it couldn't be helped. Especially on a beautiful summer's day like that.

I said I'd never forget the date of my debut. I thought it was Saturday August 18th 1958. But when I checked the stats books, it says it was August 30th. Shows how your memory can play tricks on you over time. The number 18 was big for me though as I was 18-years-old a bit.

There was nearly 14,000 at the Den for the first home game of the season. I remember running down the wing after five or ten minutes and crossing the ball. It was a lousy cross. It was going over the bar, but the goalkeeper pulled the crossbar down (like they used to do in those days) just to make sure. It was a terrible cross really, but the crowd went 'Ooh!' The fans really got behind me right from the start, which helped me settle.

About half an hour into the game, our keeper Reg Davis threw the ball out to me. I think we'd been defending a corner and I was on the edge of our box. I started running with the ball and Carlisle's full back started jockeying me. He didn't try to tackle me, he just tried to keep me hemmed in. But in the end, as I got to the edge of their box I thought: 'I'd better do something here'. He was in a position so I couldn't cross the ball. So I stopped the ball with my right foot. He stopped in his tracks. Then I knocked the ball forwards with my left foot, which created half a yard. Then I crossed it. Ronnie Heckman had come running in from the left wing to meet the cross and he whacked it into the back of the net.

The noise of our fans celebrating was dizzying to me. I suddenly didn't know where I was. Running back to the halfway line was difficult with your mind spinning like that, I

A TALE OF TWO FOOTBALL TOWNS & MILLWALL F.C.

can tell you! But I was so pumped up with adrenalin that I never stopped running until the end of the match.

It stayed 1-0 and I'd set up the only goal on my debut. So I was in a tearing hurry to buy the newspapers to see what they had to say about it. I always bought the paper for my dad anyway, but this time I bought three Saturday ones: The Standard, The News and The Star.

The best headline was the following day, when some headline writer called me "The Blonde Bombshell". My hair was quite light anyway, but with "Stay Blonde" shampoo it looked even blonder! I was only about 5 foot 2 inches or so and 9 stone 7 lbs at the time, so I needed to do what I could to make sure I didn't get over overlooked.

Anyway, everyone was patting me on the back after that performance, so I was feeling quite happy with myself. Next up, was Walsall at home on the following Monday. We'd already lost to them, so this promised to be a tough game.

And so it proved to be. We lost 3-1 and I didn't do very much at all. That's why I don't remember much about the game. But I do remember more about my first away game for Millwall. It was at Barrow. I'll tell you about it in the next chapter.

Chapter 5: After we'd lost 3-1 at home to Walsall in my second game, I wasn't necessarily expecting to be picked for the next match, which was away at Barrow on Saturday 6th September 1958.

We took the train up to Carlisle on the Friday. And from there, it was another 50 miles or so, southwest to Barrow-in-Furnace. I remember walking around the town a bit before the match. We could see the Irish Sea, but it was all shipyards and steel works really. Anyway, it was still quite relaxing at that point. I just didn't have a clue what was in store!

It's very hard to explain to your average fan how different it is playing away from home. It's like chalk and cheese. Unless you've played at these grounds, it's hard to believe how much extra energy you need to find.

So there I was running around at Barrow and my feet was aching in places they'd never ached before. I'd just run about 50 yards and that wouldn't normally tire me out that much. I'd never experienced anything like it before.

I really struggled in the game and we got whacked 3-1. After that, I was really expecting to be dropped. Luckily for me, our boss Jimmy Seed persevered with me.

The games were coming thick and fast now. We lost again, this time at home to Darlington, but then we put together an unbeaten run, beating Oldham, Darlington (away) and Gateshead before drawing with at home to Shrewsbury who ended up get promoted that season.

A TALE OF TWO FOOTBALL TOWNS & MILLWALL F.C.

Next up was Aldershot on Saturday 27th September 1958. This was significant for me because I remember crossing one in with my left foot for a Ray Brand header. Brand scored a hat-trick that day as we romped home 4-0 and I was really glad to provide him with an assist, especially as it was with my 'magic' left foot!

But not long after that game, I remember our goalkeeper, Reg Davies, starting to take "the Mickey" a bit because I still hadn't scored a goal. He became a good mate of mine though and he was well respected by the team.

A lot of the players called Reg "The Cat". Not an original name, I know, but he was at the top of his game so he deserved the moniker. So Reg was full of confidence, maybe a bit too full of it! So nothing was going to stop him pulling my leg about not scoring. So I knew I had to break my duck and the day after Reg's 25th birthday, I did it.

Now I knew how tough away games were, I wasn't expecting my first goal for Millwall to come somewhere too far from the Den. Well, it wasn't that far. It was up the road at Watford on my 'lucky' 13th game for the Lions.

My first goal was a bit of a fluke really. I ran in from the right and tried to drive in a shot. The ball deflected off the left back's toe as he tried to block it on the edge of the six-yard box. If the ball hadn't taken such a wicked deflection, I think the keeper would have saved it. He was diving the right way, but the deflected shot beat him at his near post. It was our only goal in a 1-1 draw.

I didn't score what I would call a 'proper' goal until about halfway through the season. We went up to Carlisle for our first game in 1959. I'd played 24 games by this time, and had just managed the one goal.

That day we were playing Johnny Roche at centre forward. Now Johnny had started the season playing on the right wing, but I'd come in and stolen his position after just two games. Since then, he'd only played a couple of times, yet he'd still managed to find the net three times! And he was, at Carlisle, playing a blinder, so there I was thinking I'd better buck my ideas up or otherwise he'd be replacing me in the team.

Johnny got the opening goal, so I tried my best to get on the scoresheet as well. I cut in from the right wing onto my left foot just to have a go. The goalie got his hand to it, but it just crept inside his near post for our second goal of the game and we ended up winning 2-0.

The goals started coming a lot more frequently after that, and I finished the season with 7 goals to my name. I was settling down but, as a team, we didn't exactly set the world alight that season. We finished 9th in Division Four but it was good to see another youngster making his mark.

As well as myself, my mate Dave Harper had broken through into Millwall first-team ranks. He was only 19 when he made his debut, but he played 38 games that season. They called the pair of us, the "Jimmy Seedlings". I'll tell you more about Jimmy Seed himself, in the next chapter.

A TALE OF TWO FOOTBALL TOWNS & MILLWALL F.C.

Chapter 6: To recap on the last chapter, me and my mate Dave Harper had broken through into Millwall first-team ranks and because of our age, we got called the 'Jimmy Seedlings'. Jimmy Seed, obviously, was the Millwall manager who had given both of us our debuts.

Jimmy, himself, was getting on a bit. He'd been boss at Charlton for 23 years and before that played inside right for Spurs, Sheffield Wednesday and England. He'd had a lot of success before, but now he was at Millwall for the 1958-59 season.

I remember one game in March at Hartlepools United, where we lost 3-1. I'd scored our goal. And I remember him calling me and Dave Harper into an area of the hotel we were in after the game and saying: "I made you and I'll break you." He was talking to me, but he was smelling of booze so I just walked out. Nothing ever came of it, though.

That was the sort of game we needed to win if we were going to get promoted. They were quite near the bottom, but after going 1-0 up we'd lost both points (as, of course, it was two points for a win back then). Anyway, two wins in our final twelve games was hardly promotion form and I suppose the rot started at Hartlepools. We ended up eight points off a promotion spot in ninth. In those days the top four went up automatically, but if we'd had the promotion system they use nowadays, we'd have been only one victory away from a play-off spot. So it wasn't that bad a season, overall.

I suppose we felt we should have done better, though, as when we played the teams that did well that season, like York City, who finished third, and Port Vale, the eventual champions, we whacked them at The Den. We beat Port Vale 4-2 in December and we smashed York 5-2 the month before. So you could say we had the ability, but we just hadn't delivered, especially away from home.

It was tough playing away in those days because the referees were "homers". In other words, the home side would get nine out of ten of the 50/50 decisions. Apart from that, refs were just as good back then as they are now in terms of decision-making.

I think refs were homers partly because I understand only the home team awarded the referee a mark for his performance. I remember Arthur Ellis, in particular. He was a terrible homer. He was a celebrity ref, in a way, as he'd already refereed the first ever European Cup final in 1956 and then he ended up refereeing "It's a Knockout", which was a popular TV game show in the 1970s.

Anyway, back to the managerial situation. Before my second season started, Jimmy Seed became an "advisor" at Millwall and we had a new manager: James "Cocky" Smith. Cocky was an ex-Millwall left winger. He'd been in the team that got to the FA Cup semi-final in 1937 and he'd been capped twice by England.

On the transfer front, we brought in Alf Ackerman, who was a wily old centre forward and lovely to play with. Alf joined us

A TALE OF TWO FOOTBALL TOWNS & MILLWALL F.C.

from Carlisle United, but he'd scored a lot of goals at all his previous clubs, which included: Derby County, Hull City, Norwich City and Clyde. As well as being a good player, he was a nice bloke as well.

Other pre-season signings included full back Dennis Jackson, and a couple of inside forwards in Barry Pierce and Sammy Wilson.

I reckon Cocky's best signing came the following season, when he signed Peter Burridge from Orient. He'd never done a lot for them, but he scored a lot of goals for us! Sorry, I digress!

Anyway, with the new signings, Ackerman, Jackson, Pierce and Wilson figuring right from the start of the 1959-60 season, we went unbeaten for the first 19 games.

I remember the first game of that season. We beat Workington 3-0 at The Den and we got a standing ovation from the fans. Of course, this was before all-seater stadia, so most of the supporters couldn't exactly sit and clap could they? Anyway, I knew the 13,000 or so that watched were pleased with the result and the way we'd played. That was quite clear.

So after such a great start what could go wrong? How could it all turn sour? I'll let you know in the next chapter.

Chapter 7: As I was telling you in the last chapter, we started the 1959-60 season in great form. Millwall went unbeaten for the first 19 games. It couldn't get much better than that, could it? Unfortunately, it couldn't.

We lost our first game in November, 2-1 away at Notts County and the week after that we had to play Bath City in the FA Cup first round.

We weren't too worried about the trip to Bath, although the previous year, we'd been giant-killed by a Southern League club. That time, it was Worcester City away who beat us 5-2. That came right after knocking Hitchin Town out after a first round replay. Roy Summersby's goal from the penalty spot meant we took them to The Den. In that second game against Hitchin, the final score was only 2-1, but I thought it was a comfortable win against the amateur side. Maybe it was because there were nearly 19,000 of our fans roaring us on! Anyway, we came down to earth with a bang when we got whacked by Worcester in the mud, after Johnny Roche and Alec Moyse had put us 2-1 up at half-time as well! Worcester had dominated us, so deserved their historic win.

Anyway, the following year against Bath, we were in much better form so we weren't thinking we'd go crashing out the cup so early again. I was naïve. We ended up losing 3-1. One of Bath's goals was scored by an aging former Scotland international, Charlie "Cannonball" Flemming. The 'Cannonball' lived up to his name and smacked one in from a free kick. He hit the ball so hard our wall disintegrated in front of him and our keeper had no chance.

A TALE OF TWO FOOTBALL TOWNS & MILLWALL F.C.

I hadn't done that much in the game, but I thought I'd done reasonably well in the game, despite the result.

Anyway, our boss, Cocky Smith, was going mad. He decided to show us all up by putting a cabbage on the dressing room table and he put the team sheet just below it. And then when we came in after the game, he said to us: "This cabbage has got more heart than you lot!"

It sounds quite funny now but, as a team, we weren't very happy about it at the time and stupid gestures like that made me think he wasn't a very nice bloke.

By the time of the Bath City debacle, I'd played well over 60 games for the Lions and do you know what? No one at all had given me any proper football coaching. And there I was with an ex-England winger as boss, who could have taught me a lot on the training ground. Maybe he was too busy down the greengrocers looking for vegetables in case we embarrassed ourselves again!

Back then football training was very different from nowadays. Sometimes we used to practise crossing balls, but no one told us to get to the byline and cut the ball back. The main thing we did in training was run. We'd have a practice match on a Tuesday, with the first team taking on the reserves, but that's all we used to do. Anyway, a bit of coaching wouldn't have done me any harm at all.

At the time of the Bath City defeat, I was getting near my twentieth birthday. By the end of the season, I'd knocked in

14 goals, so I hadn't done too badly and the team were pushing for promotion right until near the end.

I remember for our last home game of the season we were offered a pound-a-goal by one of the club directors for every goal we scored. That sort of bonus was illegal. It was only 1-0 to us against Chester at half-time, but we scored six more in the second half and all the team went home feeling seven quid richer! We didn't get the money until pay day the following week. Then, all of us that played in the game got an extra brown envelope to go with our normal pay packet.

Again, that season was all about what could have been. Finishing fifth in the division would mean the play-offs nowadays, but back then it meant you missed out on promotion. Maybe we just weren't quite good enough.

Although, our boss, Cocky Smith, had brought in some decent new players, we'd lost our skipper Colin Rawson to Torquay United. He was a good wing half and he ended up captaining Torquay to promotion that season.

Anyway, despite missing out on promotion ourselves, I was quite happy with life at The Den. I wasn't exactly setting the world on fire with my performances all the time, but I'd managed a decent goal return and I was a first-team fixture. I'd played two complete seasons without being dropped and now I was about to start my third campaign at Millwall. I'll tell you more about that in the next chapter.

A TALE OF TWO FOOTBALL TOWNS & MILLWALL F.C.

Chapter 8: As I was telling you in the last chapter, although Millwall missed out on promotion in the 1959-1960 season, on a personal level, things were going quite well for me at The Den. I was about to start my third campaign at Millwall and I'd still never been dropped.

Maybe our boss "Cocky" Smith thought I was getting too cocky! As next thing I knew, he was bringing in Wally Hinshelwood, a right winger from Bristol City. Now there would be competition for that coveted number 7 shirt!

Wally was a Londoner and had played for Fulham and Chelsea before. He was more than 10 years older than me, so wasn't as fast as I was, but when he beat a full back and got to the byline he would look up and cut the ball back.

Luckily for me, Millwall started playing me on the left wing and Wally took me in hand, giving me tips on how I could improve me game. He was a great bloke. And as much as the manager hated it, we used to switch wings during the game sometimes. We'd hear Cocky shouting from the sidelines: 'Don't change wings, don't change wings.' As you can imagine, that kind of talk didn't exactly inspire me. I always had the feeling that Cocky didn't like me much and he certainly didn't teach me anything of note.

Wally was the opposite of Cocky. He was always ready to pass on his football knowledge. No wonder his sons, Paul and Martin, went on to forge professional careers at Crystal Palace, the latter joining Millwall in 1984.

Wally used to talk to me and say: "This is what you've got to do." He'd explain the finer points of wing play and I used to listen to him. I have to thank him for that as he helped me to improve my game.

Despite Wally's coaching, I did get dropped early on that season. We'd only got a point from our first two games, losing away at York City and drawing at home to Accrington Stanley in front of nearly 13,000 two days later. Heads had to roll, like cabbages (see the previous installment!), and Cocky made three changes for the next game at home to Crewe Alexandra. Out went Ray Brady, Dave Bumpstead and me.

Well, initially results didn't improve. We lost 3-2 to Crewe and then we drew again with Accrington. Alf Ackerman had been wearing the number 11 shirt in my absence, but Cocky had something else up his sleeve for Chester away.

He'd brought in another young winger, a Scottish teenager called Vic Rickis, from Dalkeith Thistle. Now Cocky decided to throw Rickis in at the deep end.

Chester was quite a tough place to go as they had a decent home record and Cocky's new team stuffed them 4-1. To make my chances of getting back in the team worse, Rickis scored on his debut.

My immediate future at Millwall was looking bleak until Rickis got injured. One game and one goal and now the talented Scot was looking at spending a month on the sidelines.

A TALE OF TWO FOOTBALL TOWNS & MILLWALL F.C.

So Cocky had no choice really other than putting me back in the team against Barrow away. I ran myself into the ground and scored, but it wasn't enough. We lost 2-1. I did the same against Workington at home, but that result was even worse. A 3-0 defeat. But at least Cocky could see I was putting myself out for the team. He couldn't complain about my work rate.

Results improved a bit, but then we lost to Darlington at home and with Rickis fit again, Cocky decided to make changes. This time, Wally got the chop. I got switched to the right wing and Rickis took the number 11 shirt.

Wally, being the consummate professional he was, took getting dropped in his stride. He still got on with me, although technically I'd taken his place in the team now.

Rickis was never in a losing team at Millwall, but he only made 3 appearances in total, scoring the one goal on his debut. Wally, meanwhile, was in and out of the team from that point on.

Cocky tried a couple of other wingers out. Alan Spears, who we signed from Newcastle, had a run of games on the left wing and he weighed in with a decent goal return: 5 goals in 25 games. Not bad at all.

Brian Bevan was brought in from Carlisle United and played a few games there too. But by the end of the season, Spears was a regular and Wally was out of the picture.

Change was in the air at Millwall and I'll tell you more about it in the next chapter.

Chapter 9: As I told you in the last chapter, there was change in the air at Cold Blow Lane in 1961.

By the end of the 1960-1961 campaign, my mentor and friend, Wally Hinshelwood, had moved to Newport County. But before that happened our boss, Cocky Smith, left the club. It may have come as a bit of a shock to some people as we'd just gone 4 games unbeaten. However, in mid January of 1961, Cocky packed his bags and went off to manage some team in South Africa.

I don't really know for sure what prompted Cocky to leave. He may well have been pushed out, as I always believed he'd got the sack despite what I've read in Millwall history books since! I think the chairman, Mickey Purser, was a bit annoyed with him for dropping me. I wasn't a great player, but the Millwall crowd loved me. It may have been partly because I was a local boy, I don't know. I wasn't the finished article by any means. I was still relatively inexperienced and there were a lot of faults in my game that needed ironing out. Nevertheless, the fans had been behind me right from the start and that was still the case. They seemed disgruntled, anyway, that's for sure, and that probably was the main reason why Cocky left.

I heard that Purser said we couldn't afford to keep Cocky on. We got under 8,000 fans at the Den for Cocky's last two games in charge, so maybe the chairman had a point. Without Cocky, the supporters flooded back, despite some poor results. We got nearly 19,000 in for our final home game of the season so, in that way, Purser called it right.

A TALE OF TWO FOOTBALL TOWNS & MILLWALL F.C.

Purser could always gauge the mood of our fans. If his Old Kent Road car showroom was intact after a game, then he knew our supporters were happy. If the showroom was trashed, then clearly something had to be done!

Anyway, in January 1961, Cocky was out and in came his assistant, Ron Gray, for a second spell in charge. A couple of months after this managerial change, Ron comes in the dressing room before the Rochdale home game and says: 'A tailor in Lewisham has promised to give a new suit to anyone who scores a hat-trick.'

Most of the team didn't take a lot of notice. The only one of us likely to score a hat-trick was Peter Burridge. Peter was our top scorer, but he wasn't too keen on me. When I used to get the ball, he used to say: "Open the gates!" He thought that I used to get my head down while I was running on the wing and I wouldn't look up before crossing the ball. I was a tearaway right winger and I certainly wasn't as classy as Wally Hinshelwood, who had been coaching me.

Anyway, with the made-to-measure suit up for grabs as a prize, I got off to a great start. I scored a goal in the first 10 minutes. I smacked my shot right in the corner of the net. I have since seen a photograph of it and you can see Burridge on the ground with his hands in the air.

But then, around half-time, Dave Harper, who got married that day, got injured. Poor old Dave was always getting injured. He played over 300 games professionally, but he would have played more than 500 had he not had so many injury problems. He was a good player, so with him going off it was going to tough to add to the scoreline.

With Dave off the field, we needed to make tactical changes so I got moved from the wing to inside forward. And with about 20 minutes to go, I scored another goal to make it 2-0. Now the game felt virtually over, but the adrenalin rush I was getting from scoring twice was amazing. I was running about everywhere. With just 10 minutes left, I remember racing into the box from the halfway line and our left winger, Alan Spears, crossed. Bang! That was it! A hat-trick and a new suit!

It was one of those days. If we'd have kept playing for longer, I felt I could score six or seven. As it was, I managed to score another goal to make it 4-0. It was my only hat-trick in league football and I never ever scored three professionally . . . only four!

I always felt if I might have had a career as a striker instead of a winger. I scored loads of goals playing there for my school, Roan Grammar. Maybe I could have been another Ian Wright, who also had pace and scored so many goals for Arsenal and Crystal Palace in the 1980s and 90s. Who knows?

I can't complain really. I scored nearly 90 career goals playing on the wing. I found as I got older, I got faster running with the ball. A bit like Gareth Bale of Tottenham.

So back to Millwall, how did we finish that season under Ron Gray? And what was in store for us the following season: 1961-1962? Find out in the next chapter.

A TALE OF TWO FOOTBALL TOWNS & MILLWALL F.C.

Chapter 10: In the last chapter, I left you with two questions: how did we finish that season under Ron Gray in 1960-1961 and what was in store for us the following season? Maybe you looked up the answer in the record books, but as I've found out from my own reading, the statistics don't really tell the whole story. I will though!

When Cocky Smith left us in January, we were 8 points off a promotion place in eighth. Ron Gray took over and by the end of March, after beating Crystal Palace away in front of nearly 38,000 fans, we were in fifth and just 3 points behind fourth-placed Northampton Town. We'd won four straight games, but we just couldn't keep the run going and lost 4 of our 7 remaining games. We ended up 10 points behind the Cobblers, who finished third, level on points with fourth-placed Bradford Park Avenue.

Anyway, sixth was no disgrace and something to build on, you might say. We certainly expected better, but got off to a bad start at the beginning of the following season. We went from seventeenth at the end of August to fifth by the time we faced Third Division side, Northampton, away from home in the FA Cup. We'd been on a decent run, not losing at all in October, and we wanted to show we were just as good as one of the teams that got promoted the year before.

It wasn't to be. We lost 2-0. Back in the dressing room we were sipping beer. Northampton were good like that. They brought you beers after the game. Well, there we were sitting down contemplating what went wrong when my old mate, Reg Davies, who was playing in goal for us, started ranting and raving. Because it was him, I said: "Why don't you shut up Reg! You try playing centre forward. It ain't that easy."

His reaction was to smash an empty beer bottle on the table. Then he started going crazy. He was so upset. Then Ray Brady came over to me and said: "Shut your bloody mouth!" He was leaning over me as if he was going to bash me, so I jumped up and nutted him! They had to stitch him up, but it certainly calmed things down! Well, after a while, anyway!

Despite that setback, we weren't a bad side. The versatile Harry Obeney was playing centre forward, at the time. By mid December, he'd been switched to wing half, maybe because he hadn't scored enough goals. Our inside forwards, Peter Burridge and Dave Jones, were scoring plenty though.

Meanwhile, I'd got married and now I wasn't starting to make goals the way Wally Hinshelwood had told me I should. I was getting to the byline, looking up, and picking team-mates out. So I was playing much better. Although, I have to say I was scoring less. I only got 8 goals that season. I'd got well into double figures in the two previous seasons, but I was happy because the team were doing reasonably well.

Come the end of January, we were fourth. But Carlisle United were fifth with a game in hand and only behind us on goal average.

It was so obvious what the team needed: an out and out centre forward. I'll tell you who we recruited in next chapter.

A TALE OF TWO FOOTBALL TOWNS & MILLWALL F.C.

Chapter 11: As I was saying in the last chapter, Millwall were near the top of the league by the end of January 1962 and, to make sure we got promotion this time, what we needed was an out-and-out centre forward. Only the top four went up in those days, and that was automatic. There was no margin for error.

The answer to our problem upfront was Northampton Town striker Pat Terry. He'd asked for a move around Christmas time which was a bit surprising, given he'd only joined them during the previous summer. Northampton had paid £5,500 to Gillingham for this old-fashioned centre forward, who might have been only 5 foot 10 in height, but was still so good with his head. We knew exactly how good he was because he'd scored to help knock us out of the FA Cup, earlier that season.

So Pat Terry was in decent form. He'd already got 10 goals in 24 league games for the Cobblers so far, but he wanted out. And we needed him in. Seeing as he was a local boy, we had a good chance of landing him and that's exactly what happened. With Terry McQuade on the left wing and me on the right, as a team we thought we could provide the supply-line for Pat Terry to score us plenty of goals. We told our manager, Ron Gray, and he contacted Northampton and brought him in.

We'd just lost away at relegation-threatened Hartlepools United 2-0, but now with Pat Terry in the side, we won 3-2 at lowly Chesterfield. That victory was sweet, especially after going a goal behind. Pat Terry managed to score on his debut, but I got the winner!

Next up was Pat Terry's old club Gillingham at the Den. Nearly 15,000 turned up for a goal-less draw. We were still up near the top, but we had the likes of Aldershot, Carlisle United, York City, Crewe and Oldham all breathing down our necks.

We need a result at Crewe on Valentine's Day to pull away from the chasing pack, and Pat Terry obliged to put us 1-0 up at half-time. Sadly, we ended up losing 2-1.

But we didn't suffer too many more defeats. By early March when we played Bradford City at the Den, we couldn't really afford to slip up, but we did losing 2-1 to a team in the lower half of the table. Meanwhile, Accrington Stanley had resigned from the league for financial reasons, so all their records were expunged and obviously that affected all the other teams too.

Our next slip-up was understandable. Carlisle were fourth, so losing 3-2 there was no disgrace. But now Aldershot were five points behind, with three games in hand. Literally all the teams in the top seven hand more matches left than we did and it was very tight.

So we had to beat top-of-the-table Colchester. Nearly 17,000 expectant fans turned up at the Den and we didn't disappoint. Two goals from yours truly gave us a 2-0 victory.

By the start of April we were top of the league, level on points with Carlisle, who had played one game more than us. There was only three points separating the top five sides though, so

A TALE OF TWO FOOTBALL TOWNS & MILLWALL F.C.

we still had a lot to do to get to the finishing line. So with the pressure mounting, we travelled up to mid-table Southport and lost 3-1! And we lost top spot. Colchester moved above us and had played one game less.

Luckily, they didn't take advantage of their game in hand. By the time we were took on Barrow away in our final game of the season, we knew a draw would be enough to win us the league. Wrexham and Colchester were just two points behind and both had a better goal average, so we couldn't afford to lose.

It's a good job we drew 2-2 because Colchester smashed five past Doncaster and would have won the title instead of us had we slipped up again! Just for the record, Wrexham played a couple of days later and let five in against Bradford City. The game was already up for them and that may have affected them.

Anyway, we'd done it! At the age of 22, we'd won the league. Mickey Purser, the Millwall chairman, looked after me. Now that I was a newly-wed, I needed somewhere to live, so Purser gave me some money upfront from the benefit match I had to come. That was very kind of him.

Now I had a season in the Third Division to come with newly-promoted Millwall. And I'll tell you more about in the next chapter.

Chapter 12: As I was saying in the last chapter, Millwall won the Fourth Division in 1961-62 and now we all had a season in the Third Division to look forward to.

Looking at the stats, you can tell the signing of Pat Terry made a huge difference: 13 goals in 17 league games is a more than decent return. When you throw in Peter Burridge's 23 goals in 41 games and Dave Jones's 22 goals in 43 games you can see why we won the league. And I scored 8 that season as did Gary Townend. A great team effort!

Anyway, we were all looking forward to the opening day of the new season in a higher division away at Bristol City, just a week after my only son was born. Pat Terry scored a great headed goal to put us to 2-1 up at half-time, but Bristol City recovered to score an equaliser in front of over 14,000 fans. Pat Terry used to say to me: 'Knock the ball up between the penalty spot and the 18 yard box. Just put the ball over lovely and high so the goalkeeper thinks he can get it. But the keeper won't get it, I'll get it.'

So I tried what Pat Terry told me, just inside their half. I just lifted the ball up, lobbing it into City's penalty area. The keeper came running out to claim it, but Pat Terry got there first and headed it over him to make it 2-1 to Millwall.

For the next game we were away from home yet again. And once again we got a score draw, this time 1-1 at Port Vale. This was a decent start to the season in a very unforgiving division. With only two going up and four going down, you needed to get off to a good start. And two points from two

A TALE OF TWO FOOTBALL TOWNS & MILLWALL F.C.

games wasn't too bad at all. We were just two points behind the league leaders, Watford, who had a 100% record. And guess what? They were our next opponents at the Den.

Over 16,000 fans crammed into the Den on a very warm day in August. The highlight of the game for me was when I got the ball around about the halfway line, and started running towards the corner flag. As I was running, I noticed that I was gradually leaving the left back behind. So I cut across him, and shot at goal from about 18 yards out and to my delight it ended up in the corner of the net. We ended up winning the game 6-0. It could have been seven had the referee not disallowed goal I scored on the volley. I was a bit annoyed about that.

But what a start to the season! We'd probably started better than expected, given that we'd sold Peter Burridge to Crystal Palace during the pre-season for about £8,000. He'd left the club after that bust-up that I had in the dressing room with Reg Davies and Pat Brady the year before in the FA Cup at Northampton. That was enough for him! It was a good excuse to leave, and I can't blame him. To replace Burridge, we'd brought in Jim Towers from QPR and he'd started off well scoring a hat-trick against Watford. Jim was a good player but quite heavy, and he was reaching the tail-end of his career.

But it was so far so good. We had four points from three games and now we have to take on top-of-the-table Port Vale for the second time that season. No wonder nearly 21,000 fans turned out at the Den on the August Bank Holiday

Monday to see it. Unfortunately, it was a bit of a damp squib and we drew 0-0. That really brought us down to earth.

Now we were two points behind the new league leaders QPR, and still one point behind Port Vale, who were now in second place. Another draw followed away at Bradford but the next game was memorable one at home to Hull City. We had nearly 20,000 at the Den for that match, and I was loving it. We beat them 5-1 and I scored two on the day to take us up to third in the league table behind QPR and Southend.

Things were going well off-the-field as well. I managed to get myself a coaching job with Inner London Schools. It was good money and I used to go there 2 to 3 times a week. I used to work at William Penn School and coach the kids. You could say I was pretty happy with life.

Also, I started learning to become a cab driver. Pat Terry was doing it. A couple of the other Millwall players were doing it too. I had to learn 'The Knowledge' but it was just like learning poetry: you just had to learn it by heart.

Meanwhile, the team's form on the pitch was becoming erratic. We got hammered away at Wrexham and Peterborough and our last game before 'The Big Freeze' set in was a 3-0 Boxing Day defeat at Crystal Palace. The weather that winter was atrocious, and so was our form leading up to it. After that defeat, we were 16th in the league just one point above the drop zone, occupied by Brighton, Halifax Town, Crystal Palace and Carlisle United. So how would we fare after 'The Big Thaw? I will tell you in the next chapter.

A TALE OF TWO FOOTBALL TOWNS & MILLWALL F.C.

Chapter 13: As I was saying in the last chapter, Christmas 1962 was no time to celebrate on the field for Millwall. We lost 3-0 to Crystal Palace on a frosty Boxing Day and now we were 16th in the league, just one point above the relegation zone.

We looked at that table for nearly two months, as 'The Big Thaw' didn't kick in until mid-February. Nearly 10,000 turned up for our home game against Colchester. We won 2-1. We went on a bit of a winning streak, winning 4 out of the next 5 games, but then we lost our way a bit.

We were looking at a possible relegation after our defeat at Coventry in April. We were just 3 points off the drop zone, so we had some nervous times ahead. Four defeats in the next 5 games didn't help much. After an away defeat at Southend, we were only 2 points ahead of third-from-bottom Reading. And to make matters worse, they had a game in hand.

That was as bad as it got though and a win at QPR sparked a recovery of sorts. We ended up avoiding relegation by 3 points.

In the pre-season of 1962-3, the club decided to get rid of some of the more solid players, like Reg Davies (to Orient) and the Brady brothers (to QPR). Millwall brought in players that they thought would be better. But it doesn't always work like that.

We brought in John McLaughlin from Greenock Morton. He got off to a good start scoring two in his first three games, but only managed five career goals in total for Millwall.

We also brought in Alex Stepney from Tooting and Mitcham. Of course, Stepney went on to forge a magnificent career at Manchester United where he won the European Cup. However, at Millwall, he dropped a few clangers early on in the season. I remember him coming off his line but that was never his strong point and he made a few calamitous errors. Maybe it taught him a lesson, as he always stayed on his line at Manchester United. He was always a good shot stopper though, we could see that even then. But it took him quite a while to settle down at Millwall.

So we had this team of new faces that just wasn't gelling together. I even got moved to inside forward as the boss tinkered with the team, but that idea was abandoned and I was pushed back on the right wing.

I feel I could have done a better job as an inside forward if I had had some coaching on how to use my blistering pace. I had to work everything out for myself. I'd worked out how to use my speed on the wing but I needed more time to learn how to use it in other positions. Unfortunately, I didn't get time to learn.

I wasn't very happy so I asked for a transfer. The crowd had the hump too as we were bottom of the league, by the middle of October 1963 and I was sold to Ipswich Town for £16,000. I was going from the bottom team in the third division to the bottom team in the first division! Yet I was still excited, as Ipswich had won the league title only the year before. So what would happen to me at Portman Road? I'll tell you in the next chapter.

A TALE OF TWO FOOTBALL TOWNS & MILLWALL F.C.

Chapter 14: After playing at Millwall for five years, I thought I deserved the chance and wanted to play in the top flight. It was something I'd always dreamt of. Judging by my performances against other players, I thought I was good enough. Also, I was fed up at the time because at Millwall we were going backwards and I wanted to progress.

Apart from that, I was very happy at Millwall. They've given me a benefit (testimonial). I was on about £25 per week, and I had a good coaching job at William Penn School, which I handed on to Harry Cripps when I left. So, all in all, I was bringing in about £40 plus a week.

But the problem was we were looking like we were going to get relegated. It was depressing. I got depressed and my form got depressed as well. I wasn't playing well and I wasn't scoring goals. So I asked for a transfer and Millwall sold me for £16,000 to Ipswich Town.

So I went up to Ipswich in my lovely little Spitfire to negotiate personal terms and when I got there I was told by Ipswich boss Jackie Milburn: "We don't give out backhanders." That didn't put me off because I didn't care less about the money. I just wanted to play in the first division.

Jackie was a lovely bloke and a football legend, but I was a bit disappointed upon meeting him as he said: "Joe, when I've watched you play you haven't done that well. But I've been told I must sign you by other people." I didn't get annoyed because he said everything in such a nice way, but I couldn't help but feel a bit deflated.

Jackie had probably taken the advice of Jim "Chisel" Forsyth - who had played a couple of hundred games for Millwall before the war, but now was the trainer (coach) at Ipswich. I'm pretty sure that Chisel had watched me a few times at Millwall and he had kept in good contact with his old friends down at The Den, so he knew a fair bit about me. Unfortunately, Jackie seem to know a lot less.

I was quite excited, though, about the prospect of joining the league champions of a couple of seasons ago. Ipswich had won the first division in 1961-1962, the same season Millwall had won the fourth division. Now just 18 months on from those magic moments, Ipswich were bottom of the first division and Millwall were bottom of the third division. Still, with Ipswich's pedigree I wasn't so sure they would be relegated. And even if they did go down, I would still get a taste of top-flight football.

Ipswich's plight did not seem that perilous. After 13 games they had four points, but were only 3 points behind third-from-bottom Birmingham, who had a game in hand. Only two teams went down in those days.

Ipswich had finished sixth from bottom in the previous season, and Jackie had only presided over the last four games of the season, when Alf Ramsey left to take over the England job. Jackie had done okay initially: winning one, drawing two and losing one. Alf had been on the way out since October 1962 to ensure smooth handover. By the end of the season, Ipswich had only slipped down one place in the league table so perhaps the transition was as smooth as it could get.

A TALE OF TWO FOOTBALL TOWNS & MILLWALL F.C.

Anyway, I just wanted to play all these top grounds, like Old Trafford, Anfield, White Hart Lane, Highbury, St James's Park and so on. But my first game for Ipswich was at Bloomfield Road, Blackpool. Not the biggest of grounds, admittedly, but just to put things in context, my previous game for Millwall was a home defeat against Peterborough United in front of less than 9,000 fans on October 14th 1963. Now that I had jumped up two divisions, I was playing away at Blackpool in front of nearly 15,000 supporters, just five days later.

The biggest change, however, was that attitude of the home fans. I'd been used to Millwall's fanatical fans. They could be stroppy and, of course, when I asked for a transfer they weren't too pleased and I got booed a few times. And if they didn't think you were having a go they could ruin you as a player. But, all in all, they were brilliant. The noise they made when you scored a goal inspired me.

The Ipswich fans were very different. They were lovely people, but they were so quiet. You could almost hear a mouse or a pin drop. They would cheer if you made a cross, but there was no real passion like you'd get at Millwall. In a way, that was a good thing because you didn't feel under so much pressure.

The biggest difference, though, was the pitch. The playing surface at Portman Road was wonderful. Town didn't play on it much, as there was a practice pitch around the back of one of the stands.

The practice pitch was not that good. It was a bit like Millwall's pitch: tight and bumpy. The first-team pitch at Portman Road was so superb that it used to be a cricket ground. Even Georgie Best said that was the best pitch he'd ever played on. For someone like me, who liked to run with the ball, it was a blessing to be able to do that on a flat surface rather than on cobblestones, if you know what I mean.

Anyway, I signed on the dotted line for Ipswich Town and now I was on £35 per week with a nice semi-detached house to live in. But before I could settle into my new home, I was on the train with the rest of the team up to Blackpool.

That was when I noticed how different things were at Ipswich. We arrived in Blackpool on the Friday night, and some of the team said to me: "Come on Joe, are you coming out for a pint?" I couldn't believe it. The night before the match and here we were going out on the lash. All of them had two or three pints each. It was virtually the team that had won the league, minus Ray Crawford, who'd been sold to Wolves. Also out was Roy Bailey. He was an excellent keeper and his son, Gary, went on to forge a decent career with Manchester United. I think Roy was injured as he returned to the team shortly after that game. Larry Carberry was the other championship winner who missed the Blackpool trip. I'll tell you what happened at Bloomfield Road in the next chapter.

A TALE OF TWO FOOTBALL TOWNS & MILLWALL F.C.

Chapter 15: So here I was at Bloomfield Road on Saturday 19th October 1963 ready to make my debut for the English League champions of 1962: Ipswich Town. Unfortunately, we needed points desperately, as we were bottom of the league. Instead of points, we'd had pints in the pub the night before, but it didn't stop us picking up an extra point at Blackpool's expense!

It finished 2-2 with Baxter and Hegan on the scoresheet, and at I remember that at half-time I had a stiffness in my shinbone, which was painful. Other than that, I was quite happy with how the game had gone. We'd lost every single away game bar one up until the Blackpool trip, so it was a triumph of sorts! I hadn't really contributed much, but it was great to be involved.

Next up with Liverpool at Portman Road. This was going to be even tougher, as the Reds were only 2 points off top spot. So we've kicked off in front of just over 16,000 fans and as I'm running with the ball I've noticed I don't have just one player marking me. Liverpool's left winger, Peter Thompson, was helping the left back to deal with me. I couldn't believe it, as he was chasing back all the time. With a work-rate like that, no wonder he ended up playing for England!

Anyway, Liverpool took the lead, but I managed to escape Thompson's attentions, for a moment, to cut the ball back to Hegan, who whacked it in to make it 1-1. So I was chuffed as I'd made a goal. In the end, it didn't affect the result as Liverpool snatched a winner but, reflecting on my own performance, I thought I'd done alright. They didn't call me "greedy Joey Broadfoot" for nothing. I had a bit of a selfish streak you might say but, of course, I wanted the team to do well.

That wasn't happening. We lost the next game at Nottingham Forest 3-1 and then our plight was rubbed in our faces by Stoke City, who ran out 2-0 winners at Portman Road.

Our return game against Stoke wasn't until March, but it was quite eventful for me, as I got put on the left wing. That meant I was right opposite the legendary Stanley Matthews. I'd watched him from the stands 10-15 years before, but I'd never been as close as this. He didn't shake hands, as not many players did that back then, but he nodded to me before kick off.

They scored first, but after about 15 minutes a long ball was sent forward for me to chase. It was a very muddy pitch and I chased it like mad. The old Victoria Ground had a bit of a slope and we were kicking uphill, so the ball held up a bit. I got there before anyone else. I was just outside the penalty area slightly to the left. I saw the keeper on his line. I hit it with my left foot first time and it flew in. It was one of the best goals I ever scored. Lawrie Leslie was in goal for them and he ended up playing at Millwall with me a few years later.

I thought things couldn't get much better than that. I'd scored my first away goal for Ipswich and now we were level. But Stoke went and ruined it by scoring 9. We'd let in 10 earlier in the season, so I couldn't believe we'd gone and done it again!

A TALE OF TWO FOOTBALL TOWNS & MILLWALL F.C.

Another game that sticks out in my memory from that season was our Friday night game against West Ham United at Portman Road, just before Christmas. It was snowing! It was a lovely blanket of snow on the pitch and we're running around and before we know it we're 2-0 down against a star-studded team, including Bobby Moore, Geoff Hurst, Martin Peters and so on. They were all out there.

You might say it wasn't looking good. We hadn't won a game since I'd arrived: we'd lost 6 and drawn 3 if you must know, and here we were up against the elements as well as a talented team.

We had some hope though, in the form of Gerry Baker, a recent signing from Hibernian. His brother, Joe, played for Arsenal, but Gerry was also a lively centre forward. He knew where the back of the net was, that was for sure.

Anyway, right after half time we pulled a goal back. That lifted us. Then we got the equaliser and somehow we even managed a winner. I didn't score in that game, but I remember putting in a couple of decent crosses which led to goals. I think Gerry scored his goal that night from one of my crosses.

It was my first win as an Ipswich player and what a way for it to happen! An early Christmas present, if you like, and against all odds made the points all the more precious.

So we've had a lovely Christmas and now we've got Fulham away on Boxing Day. I remember our boss, Jackie Milburn, giving us a team talk at Craven Cottage. He was telling one of our Scottish defenders to mark Fulham's Scotland international forward, Graham Leggat. Our guy said to Jackie: "I'll have him in my pocket, boss". Leggat scored four goals and he was a right winger normally. With Alan Mullery, who went to greater success at Spurs, they murdered us 10-1.

It was so frustrating. Jackie told me that he didn't want me back in our half, probably because he thought I couldn't defend very well. But it's about getting bodies back, it's not always about defending as such. You stop the flow of the service if you check back, as another Ipswich manager, Bill McGarry, later told me. I'd seen Thompson do that against us for Liverpool, so why couldn't I do it for Ipswich?

It wasn't all bad for me though. Fulham were so far in front that they didn't bother marking tightly, so I kept getting the ball and racing past their England international left back, Jimmy Langley. "Gentleman Jim" was getting on a bit and the muddy conditions suited me, so I kept crossing the ball in. Finally, I tried a shot that the goalie parried and Gerry Baker slid in the rebound.

From a personal point of view, I'd had a good game despite the result. A famous DJ on Radio Luxembourg, called Pete Murray, told me I'd played well that day, when I picked him up in my taxi one night. He'd recommended me to Arsenal boss Billy Wright, he said.

So what would happen? Find out in the next chapter.

A TALE OF TWO FOOTBALL TOWNS & MILLWALL F.C.

Chapter 16: Last time I left you with a bit of a cliffhanger, didn't I? What would happen after DJ Pete Murray recommended me to Arsenal? The answer to that is nothing happened, to my knowledge. Of course, things go on behind the scenes at clubs that players are not always aware of, so for all I know Arsenal did make a bid for me and it was turned down. Something like that did happen to me, but I'll come to that later.

I also told you about Ipswich's 10-1 mauling at Craven Cottage. That was the stuff horror movies, apart from on a personal level, as I'd performed quite well despite the result.

We had a team meeting before our next game, which was against Fulham again, only two days later. This time we had home advantage, but we'd need it after such a heavy defeat!

Our boss Jackie Milburn took us for a walk along the sea front at Felixstowe. It's all stones for those of you that haven't been there. A sort of Brighton without the nudists and the Taj Mahal. It was a lovely day and I remember the manager saying: "Don't listen to Joe if he's going to moan about everything. We'll go out there with the same team." And we did more or less. Danny Hegan came in for Ted Phillips, but that was the only change.

Can you believe it? we beat Fulham 4-2. I scored my first goal at Portman Road, so it was a good day all round. It was a really unusual goal. I ran after the ball. The Gibraltarian Tony Macedo was in goal for Fulham, I think. He came running out to pick the ball up and I ran past him. He turned with the ball in his hands looking for a team-mate to distribute to, but he the same way as me. Then he dropped the ball. He dropped the ball at my feet. I couldn't miss. But what a strange goal!

We went two goals up in this game, but they pegged us back to 2-2. Then, I had a shot near the end of the game. Macedo parried it and Gerry Baker whacked in the rebound and we ended up winning 4-2.

Once we went ahead again, I was scared they'd call the game off. It suddenly got foggy, so it was a possibility that they'd abandon the game.

Next up, for our first game of 1964, it was the third round of the FA Cup. We had a potentially tricky tie looming against promotion-chasing Oldham Athletic, who were two divisions below us but not that many league places separated us, as they were third and we were bottom.

Any worries were needless. I scored within about two minutes and we went on to win the game 6-3, with Baker scoring a hat-trick and Hegan a brace. It was a good result, but one thing that annoyed was how the Oldham players got away with repeatedly kicking lumps out of me during the game. In those days, you got no protection from referees.

So I got fed up with it. We were about 5-2 up at the time and, being the nasty chap that I am, I casually walked past the Oldham left back while the ball was somewhere else and I whacked him in the stomach. He went down, but he got up and chased after me like he was going to kill me. I was running all over the pitch and this full back was chasing me. It

A TALE OF TWO FOOTBALL TOWNS & MILLWALL F.C.

must have looked really funny and the referee didn't even seem to notice.

In the end, he got fed up chasing me. In those days, I was so quick that no one could catch me.

On the Monday following, I received a letter from a fan. It said: "We don't do that sort of thing up here at Ipswich." I thought it was funny, but I thought I'd better behave myself from now on. Well, at least I would while I was at Ipswich.

I had a lot of respect for the club and in particular the chairman. Mr John [Cobbold] was marvelous. He never interfered and there was never any extra pressure put on the team.

It was completely different at Millwall. I liked the chairman there as Mickey Purser was good to me, but he used to put the team under pressure. He'd come into the dressing room and say things like: "Must win today lads."

By contrast, Mr John would say: "My only problem is if we run out of wine in the board room." I think that's why Ipswich were generally successful under his chairmanship. Mr John would leave everything to the manager. He left the manager to get on with his job. Of course, that's fine when you've got somebody like Alf Ramsey at the helm, but not so clever if your manager isn't managing that well.

Jackie Milburn was a nice man, but he had a habit of saying silly things to the team and he never mentioned anything to us about tactics. I don't think he was that strong as far as recruitment was concerned. There were maybe five players in our Division One team who would have really struggled to get into Millwall's Division Three side. That Ipswich team let in 121 goals that season. Statistically, we had the worst defence by far and sometimes statistics don't lie. Then again, you do have to defend from the front, so it's unfair to just blame the defence for goals conceded. In football, if everyone gets behind the ball, it's much harder for teams to break you down. If you allow good teams space they will rip you to pieces. And that's what happened. We had no tactics and that's what I put our defensive frailties down to.

I was happy enough on a personal level, as I was given licence to fly down the wing. But although temporarily we were looking a better team after two home wins, I soon got fed up again as we failed to win another game in January.

All the while, I was jumping into my little sports car and taking myself back down to London. I was doing "The Knowledge", so I could become a fully-fledged black taxi driver. I had to go back once a month at the beginning and then that became once a fortnight. Most people would learn it from driving around on a scooter, but I did mine in a Triumph Spitfire.

I did it because I had nothing else to do. You don't have much to do as a footballer as, in those days, I didn't play golf. Anyway, driving a cab appealed to me.

So I drove down to a place in Islington, run by the police, to get examined on "The Knowledge". I've gone down there in early 1964 and this examiner says to me: "I saw you play at

A TALE OF TWO FOOTBALL TOWNS & MILLWALL F.C.

Fulham. I thought you did very well. Pity about the rest of the team."

I said: "Thank you, sir? If you like football, would you like a cup final ticket?"

He replied: "I must pay for it."

"Okay, I'll sell you it for a fiver."

I got given two tickets by Ipswich so, next time I saw this examiner, I sold him the ticket just before he tested me. He asked me: "Can you take me from Charing Cross to Euston?" It was a simple question and even simpler questions followed.

Then he said: "Okay, you've passed." Then he told me to work on my knowledge of the suburbs and come back.

I did that and I saw him a couple more times. I had to take a taxi driving test and next thing I knew I had my cab driver's licence. Then I knew I'd never be skint.

London and General was the company I started with. You just pick out a cab and away you go. When you bring the cab back you pay them half what's on the clock roughly. And you keep your tips. You didn't even have to pay for petrol or insurance. It was a good living.

But long term, it was hard work because of the traffic in London and some of the people you meet. Every now and then you meet a "wrong 'un".

It's back to football in the next chapter as I'll be talking about what happened following our relegation from Division One with Ipswich.

A TALE OF TWO FOOTBALL TOWNS & MILLWALL F.C.

Chapter 17: As promised, it's back to football, in this chapter, as I tell you what happened at Ipswich following our relegation from Division One.

I'd settled in quite well and had scored a few goals at the end of my first ever season in Division One, so I was quite happy at Ipswich despite our relegation. I've got to credit a lot of those goals to Town's left winger, Jimmy Leadbetter. You'd make a run into the box and he'd cross the ball so it would land right in front of you. He could put goals on a plate for you. I wished I'd had the chance to play with players like that when I was younger and fitter.

Anyway, I was feeling quite full of myself and it was obvious we were going to relegated so I went to see our boss Jackie Milburn and asked for a transfer.

Jackie said: "Please don't ask for a transfer. You'll get me the sack!" He was nearly in tears.

The only reason I'd asked for a transfer was so I could spend more time in London driving my cab, so I replied: "Okay, I'll carry on playing for you, but I'm not staying up here in Ipswich. I'm going back to London."

Although I left a lovely house behind in Ipswich, I was happy to be back in London, driving my cab all summer. My next action on the pitch would be the opening game of the 1964-65 season, away at Cardiff City. I'll never forget because I picked up the first-team kit in my black taxi. I put the kit bag in the basket next to me, but I didn't bother strapping it in and as I went around a corner at Hyde Park, all the kit fell out into the road. There were football boots in there as well. Ipswich's trainer Jimmy Forsyth was with me and he said: "What are you doing?" But we gathered it all up and caught a train to Cardiff.

We ended up getting a creditable 0-0 draw at Ninian Park, in front of nearly 17,000 fans. A good start to the season, apart from my kit accident!

On the way back after the match, guess what Jackie Milburn said? He said: "We'll be top of the league next Saturday." I could understand him being a little bit elated, but we had a home game against Coventry to negotiate first on Tuesday night.

Of course, Jackie's words jinxed us. We were on top of Coventry for the first 20 or so minutes, but we didn't score. Then they went in front and settled down. Coventry ended up winning quite comfortably 3-1.

Next it was Preston North End at Portman Road. They completely murdered us and, with their wingers doing most of the damage, they won 5-1.

So Jackie's confident prediction had backfired. After 3 games played, we were second-from-bottom with only Crystal Palace below us. And things weren't going to get better any time soon.

Next up was Coventry away. We let in five at Highfield Road in a 5-3 defeat. We lost our local 'derby' to Norwich by a single

A TALE OF TWO FOOTBALL TOWNS & MILLWALL F.C.

goal and we had to wait until the last Saturday in September for our first win.

Just before that victory in the league, we played Coventry in the League Cup. I hardly got a kick of the ball in the first half so I had the right hump. Just to stir things up in the dressing room, I said to the Scottish Catholics in our team: "Why ain't you passing me the ball? Is it because I'm Protestant?" I was only joking, but they went bananas! Luckily, I didn't say stupid things like that very often!

Anyway, the upshot of that poor run of results was Jackie Milburn resigned in early September. Ipswich didn't sack him, but he walked. He was a smashing bloke, but not a very good manager, sadly. It was a shame we'd got off to such a lousy start, especially as Jackie had brought in some good players though, like Frank Brogan from Celtic and Mick McNeil. One of the first games after Jackie resigned was away at Mick's old club, Middlesbrough.

It was 2-2 and I scored to put us in front and then Frank scored to make it 4-2, which was how it ended. Our first win of the season came away from home! We couldn't believe it. Jimmy Forsyth was in charge now. He was our caretaker boss, so we were quite surprised to see Jackie in the dressing room after the game. He was working as a newspaper reporter now for the Newcastle Chronicle or something. Anyway, Jackie came in and said: "Why didn't you play like that for me?" It was as if he thought we'd all let him down. We didn't know what to say.

Of course, Jackie will always be a hero for his exploits as a player, and quite rightly so. I thought journalism suited him better than management as, although he wasn't good at winning matches, he was and is a football legend and everyone wanted to hear his views.

Anyway, around about the time of the Middlesbrough game, I sustained an injury. It was a light tear in my thigh muscle. Every time I'd sprint, I'd get twinges. It was affecting my game a bit.

By October, something else would happen that would affect my game. And I'll tell you about it in the next installment.

So it's October 1964, and here I am at Ipswich Town playing in Division Two. I forgot to mention, thanks to our relegation I'd now played in all four divisions.

With the departure of Jackie Milburn, our form had improved and we were starting to compete but we were still second-from-bottom. Then our new boss arrived. It was Bill McGarry from Watford.

Like Jackie, Bill had played for England, but that's where the similarity ended. Bill had a tough reputation and had done very well at Bournemouth as player-manager before moving on to take charge of the Hornets. They used to be a soft touch and one of teams we used to love to play, when I was at Millwall, but that changed once McGarry took over. I remember they beat us 3-0 at the Den once. That was unimaginable before the McGarry era.

A TALE OF TWO FOOTBALL TOWNS & MILLWALL F.C.

Would he transform us too? Well, I thought he might do. He kept things simple and he made us train hard. Yet he made training interesting as well.

For matches, he employed different tactics which varied according to the opposition. Sometimes he'd say: "We ain't going to go for it, we're just going to play tight. Work hard as a unit." That kind of thing. "If we go 2 down, we might change it, but unless we do we've always got a chance of getting back in it."

It seemed to work. His training methods got us fitter and his team selection improved us too. He brought in Cyril Lea, who was a really good player. He used to get the ball and play a simple pass to me. Then I could take it and run towards the corner flag. I preferred those passes to feet instead of those hopeful balls that I'd have to chase. That would waste my energy.

That kind of football was attractive to the fans and enjoyable for the players. If I was on song, it made me look a much better player in a team that played this way. I was a hit or miss most of the time. I couldn't have done too badly, as a lot of people recognised me, at that time. At my best, I must have made a good impression.

I'd not done well enough to be recognised by the England selectors, unfortunately. However, McGarry said to me: "If I'd have got hold of you a couple of years earlier, you'd have played for England." That was a very nice thing for him to say.

Anyway, when he arrived we were still down the bottom of the league. But guess where we ended up? Fifth! And that season was the best I'd ever played.

I remember cutting inside from the right wing against Newcastle at Portman Road, and causing them a lot of problems. That was just before McGarry's arrival. Newcastle were top of the league and ended up clinching the title, so to beat them 3-1 was some achievement. My performance that day must have been reasonably good because their left back Frank Clark (who later went to win European Cup winners medals with Nottingham Forest) was going on about it nearly 10 years later. Frank was asked by the Soccer Star Magazine in the mid 1970s who was the best winger he ever played against. He replied: "You've probably never heard of this bloke, but it was Joe Broadfoot of Ipswich." I was really chuffed with that complement.

I wasn't so cuffed when I met Frank Clark in Nottingham in or around the year 2000. I said: "I'm Joe Broadfoot. Thanks for saying that Frank. You know, about me being the best winger you ever played against."

He looked at me like he didn't recognise my name or know what I was talking about. He'd obviously completely forgotten about it.

I saw the article because someone brought it down to Old Roan club one night. That was a cause for celebration, not that we needed a lot of excuses to neck a couple more pints!

In the next chapter, I'll tell you about the events of 1966.

A TALE OF TWO FOOTBALL TOWNS & MILLWALL F.C.

Chapter 18: Okay, where was I? Oh yeah, I promised to let you know what happened in 1966, the year England won the World Cup. It was quite eventful for me on a professional level too, but I'll come to that later.

To set the scene, more or less as soon as Bill McGarry arrived as the new boss of Ipswich in October 1964, I wanted to see him in his office. I knew he was a miserable so-and-so but, as I knew Crystal Palace were interested in me, I still plucked up the courage to say: "I wouldn't mind a transfer."

He replied: "Give us a chance."

Then I said: "But you're such a miserable bastard."

And he came back with: "What have I got to be happy about? Have you seen the players we've got here?"

I could see his point. We had over 40 players, I think, and over 30 of them were Scotsmen. Most of them had not done much in Scotland, so what were the chances they were going to do better in a tougher league south of the border? As well as that, the two trainers were Scottish. Most of them had been recruited by our previous boss, Jackie Milburn.

Anyway, McGarry sorted things out, taking us to 5th in the league after a really poor start under Milburn. By the summer of 1965, McGarry was pleased with me and I was pleased to be playing for him at Ipswich.

So I came up to Ipswich for pre-season training and stayed in a hotel for a few days, as I always did now I was based in London, thinking everything in the garden was rosy.

Then along came Sammy Chung as McGarry's number two. Not to put too fine a point on it, Sammy got on my nerves. Sammy was always trying to push you. When I was playing, I hated to be nagged by the coach, who might tell me to get back to mark their winger. I'd prefer to be told before the game what the management team wanted of me, as then I would try to work it into my game. But when I was jogging back and Sammy was shouting: "C'mon Joe, get back, get back," it was more than I could take.

I just shouted back: "For f**k's sake, Sammy, shut up, will you?" He didn't do it anymore, after that.

The truth was I wasn't playing very well. One reason I wasn't doing all that well was I missed a week of pre-season training because I didn't feel like it! Having my black taxi cab gave me a certain amount of independence and meant I didn't have to toe the line as much. I was a bit of a character, you might say, and they'd have to put up with me!

Anyway, it wasn't just me that was under-performing. The team were too. By 13th November 1965, we were 15th. A far cry from last season's 5th-placed finish.

So suddenly, I wasn't as happy as before at Ipswich and, to compound matters, something happened when I was playing cricket for the Old Roan during the summer. Crystal Palace's experienced forward Ronnie Allen was playing for opposition.

A TALE OF TWO FOOTBALL TOWNS & MILLWALL F.C.

I'd remembered playing against him at football because he was always making comments like: "Take it easy, Joe, we're going to buy you next week."

Ronnie was later to become manager of Wolverhampton Wanderers, but I wasn't to know that at the time. Anyway, we got talking. as you do, over a pint after the cricket match, and he said: "Would you be interested in joining Wolves?" I think he was assistant boss at the time, I'm not sure. He could have just been chief scout, I don't know.

I said: "I've got a cab and a little house in London, so I don't know. I'm pretty happy."

And I was. Ipswich had treated me so well. They'd taken all the players and their wives away on a Mediterranean cruise and we'd all enjoyed it. We'd also toured Norway. I felt so at ease with the club and, especially the chairman Mr John [Cobbold]. Mr John was a bit eccentric, just like me. We even used to play chess together! I was at the peak of my career and when you're a star at a good club it's a great feeling.

And I had my cab. I could go to work at any time in that. Even Christmas Day. If I got bored, I went to work. So I had plenty of money and I was famous with a good family life too, so why would I want to change anything?

But Ronnie Allen said to me: "Would £3,000 tempt you to come to Wolves?" That was the equivalent of at least £300,000 nowadays. To put it in perspective, my little house in East Dulwich cost less than Ronnie was offering.

I said: "I'd go to the moon for £3,000."

And he said: "Don't ask for a transfer. Just sit tight and we'll buy you."

So I waited at Ipswich. But nothing happened. Wolves' interest did affect my form, though. Now I just started going through the motions when I was playing. Something was missing.

I waited some more and, in November 1965, McGarry wanted a word with me. I was expecting to hear that Wolves had made a bid for me. But I was surprised when McGarry said: "Would you like to go to Northampton and talk to them? We've agreed a price to sell you."

Now, at this time, Northampton were a Division One side who had just come up through the leagues in a very short space of time. They'd got promoted from Division Four in 1960-61 and consolidated the following year before winning Division Three in 1962-63. A year of consolidation followed again before promotion from Division Two as runners-up. This was the Cobblers first ever season in the top flight and I now had the chance to be a part of it their fight to stay in it. Although, they were bottom of their division, but weren't cut adrift. They had a reasonable chance of staying up.

So I said to McGarry: "I'll go and talk to them." I didn't like the sound of it, though. I'd played at Northampton before and I'd never impressed. I had scored there, but hadn't done much else. The County Ground was also used for cricket, like Portman Road, but it wasn't such a good playing surface.

A TALE OF TWO FOOTBALL TOWNS & MILLWALL F.C.

Good enough for Northampton Cricket Club to play there in the summer though.

So I drove up to Northampton in my little Spitfire to meet the Cobblers boss, Dave Bowen. Dave had brought the club secretary along with him for this meeting in a local hotel bar.

The first thing he said to the secretary was: "Give Joe £200."

I couldn't believe it. That was a lot of money in those days. So I took it.

Dave continued: "I want you here at Northampton. How much do you want to sign on?"

I said: "Well, I was offered £3,000 by Wolves."

He replied: "I'm not giving you that much. I'll give you £2,000."

Dave could see I was a bit disappointed, so he added: "Go back to Ipswich and ask them to give you some of the transfer fee. You've done ever so well for them and we're giving them £27,000 for you, so you're entitled to a few bob."

So I said: "Okay".

But I didn't ask Ipswich for any money. That was partly because I owed the chairman, Mr John [Cobbold], £50. I'd borrowed some money from him and hadn't paid it back yet.

Anyway, to cut a long story short, I signed for Northampton. It was the worst thing I ever did. I only went there for the money.

I wonder how it would have worked out had I had got the chance to go to Wolves. I found later that they'd bid £40,000 for me that summer, but Ipswich had rejected it.

On the plus side, I got another crack at playing in top flight. We took on Spurs at the County Ground on my debut on 20th November 1965, but we lost 2-0 in front of nearly 18,000 fans.

I don't like talking or writing about my time at Northampton because I didn't perform up to the expectations of the fans and management after leaving Ipswich Town to join them. They paid a record fee for me and I just couldn't live up to it, no matter how hard I tried.

I think if I could have taken the Portman Road pitch with me I may have played better as the Suffolk turf suited my style of play. I used to like to run with the ball and it's easier to do this on a carpet than on cobblestones. This is a fact not an excuse. One game against Manchester United against George Best, Bobby Charlton and their other legends is all I remember. I was too fast for Noel Cantwell and the United manager Matt Busby swapped the full backs over in the second half.

Graham Moore played really well against his old club and hit some lovely long balls to the corner flag for me to chase but we still lost 6-2. We did beat Leeds 2-1 at home, but at Christmas time we lost twice to Chelsea 1-0. Bobby Tambling

A TALE OF TWO FOOTBALL TOWNS & MILLWALL F.C.

scoring in both games late on. I was not enjoying my football for the reasons already given and when I had to have stitches above my eye after an attack on me by a drunken team mate, that was it. The final straw. I played my last game for the club in a 3-1 away defeat against Sheffield Wednesday. We were third from bottom now, but the two teams in the relegation zone (Fulham and Blackburn) had games in hand.

But I didn't really care anymore. I felt the manager didn't like me anymore after I missed a sitter in one of our away games. He'd had me in for extra tackling training with John Kurilla and now I was completely demoralised.

I went back to London and drove my black cab again. The board contacted me and asked me to come in for a meeting. I explained my point of view to them, regarding the incident where I got whacked by a team-mate. They said I'd wound him up.

But I was back in the manager's plans after that meeting, as he asked me to play against Spurs at White Hart Lane. I stayed in a London hotel with the rest of the team on the Friday night before the match on Saturday 16th April 1966. We were just outside the drop zone: three points ahead of Fulham, who still had two games in hand. Of course, it was only two points for a win in those days.

In short, we needed every point we could get. But in order to play, I needed boots. When we arrived at White Hart Lane, I realised I'd left my boot behind at the hotel. I asked Dave

Bowen if I should get a taxi back to pick them up. He said: "Don't bother."

I stayed on the bench and shouted encouragement. We got a 1-1 draw and a point, but now Fulham had closed the gap to two points. We were playing them next at the County Ground.

Once again, Dave Bowen opened the door for me to resurrect my Northampton career, but once again unseen forces closed it. As I was still based in London, I decided to drive up to Northampton on the day of the game. Unfortunately, my car conked out on the way and I found myself stuck in Luton. I decided to watch Luton Town, who were playing that day, as I knew I'd never make it to our match in time.

Northampton lost 4-2. The result meant Fulham leapfrogged above us and we were plunged into the relegation zone with just two games to go. But it wasn't "we" anymore, it was "them".

Northampton beat Sunderland 2-1 in their last home game to move up to 18th in the league table, but all the teams below had games in hand. Northampton needed to win their last game away at Blackpool, but they lost 3-0.

They were relegated to Division Two at the end of the season and I was sold to Millwall, who had just been promoted for two seasons running. England won the World Cup during that summer of 1966 and I was back home playing for the Lions again.

A TALE OF TWO FOOTBALL TOWNS & MILLWALL F.C.

It must be remembered in those days I could earn nearly as much driving a taxi as you could playing football. This enabled me to do the things I did. Also, unlike today's game which would have made me a millionaire, £20-30 plus a week didn't inspire you to look after yourself physically or to work at improving skills.

I was never coached by anyone and therefore never made the most of my natural ability. I used my pace off the mark to kick the ball past the full back and run. It was an easy and simple way to play and it worked brilliantly for me at Ipswich, on the pitch that George Best said was the best he'd ever played on. We did have a practice pitch on the other side of the stand, so that the playing surface was only used on match days. That beautiful pitch was the result of tender loving care.

The only thing I ever practiced was shooting with my left foot. Consequently I scored more league goals (over fifty) with my swinger than I did with my natural right foot. Not having worked at improving my game didn't help me at Northampton and in a poor team I have to admit I was a poor player.

Now I'll tell you a bit more about the incident that ended my time at Northampton. After it, I needed stitches in a wound above my eye, so I was pretty shook up by what had happened.

I'd gone out on a Tuesday night with the rest of the Northampton players for a drink. One of the players, let's call him Mr X, asked me to give him a lift to a party. I said okay, but I was bit perplexed because Mr X brought two girls along for the ride and I only had a Triumph TR4, a sports car. When Mr X started slapping one of the girls around in my car, I stopped driving and then I threw him out. I took the two girls on to the party. I had a drink while I waited for Mr X to arrive at the party but, when he came in, he nutted me. Mr X was still in a drunken rage. He caught me by surprise and he cut my eye open. That's why I needed stitches. What annoyed me most of all was that he lost control completely and kept trying to head-butt me for ages until the other lads calmed him down.

There were more shocks and surprises in store for me in 1966 and I'll tell you more in the next chapter but, before that, here are some other points of view on what went wrong for Northampton Town?

Theo Foley, right back: "Northampton Town waited too long to sign players who had played in Division One before and who could handle that level of football, like Graham Moore, the ex-Chelsea and Manchester United player. Plus we had some bad luck in at the beginning of the season. I also felt that the players, who had done so well for the club in the past, could not help one another as much as they had done. The club itself was not geared up for Division One. We'd made wonderful progress in a short time, so it was wonderful to be there."

Frank Grande, Northampton Town football historian: "I believe Northampton went down because they went up too fast. From Division Four to Division One in five seasons meant

A TALE OF TWO FOOTBALL TOWNS & MILLWALL F.C.

there was no stability. If we had gone up at a slower pace, then they may have stayed in the higher sphere.

"We also had no strength in depth. Injuries to key players meant putting youngsters in and, although we had a great crop of youngsters, they were being thrown into the lion's den.

"There was a certain amount of bad luck, losing centre half Terry Branston, and inspirational skipper, Theo Foley, for part of the 1965-66 season, but that's football!

"Dave Bowen was an astute businessman. He made all his own money for the transfer market by picking up players for next to nothing and selling them on for high fees. He also believed in the youth policy and, it is fair to say, that the youth and reserve team were at their strongest under Dave Bowen.

"He had an eye for raw talent and tried to bring Francis Lee, Alex Stepney, Colin Bell and Mike England to Northampton Town while they were still raw youngsters. However, the directors would not cough up the money and all those players went on to represent their country.

"Dave was not the most popular man amongst the players, but then the boss never is. He was a wheeler dealer and made around a quarter of a million pounds profit for the club in his days as club manager.

"I don't think he ever changed his style, he always went for attacking football hence the amount of strikers he bought.

"The turning point was the 1965-66 season. The club, not the team, were not ready for Division One football. There was little or no money available to strengthen the team and, if someone was signed, another player had to go. Yet only on a few occasions were the team completely outplayed. They held their own against most Division One opponents.

"I don't remember the head-butting incident involving Joe Broadfoot and another player at Northampton, but there were some unsavoury moments during the 1965-66 season. We had some very talented players, like Barry Lines and Joe Kiernan, but sometimes they were kicked all over the park. So the side also included players like John Kurilla and Mike Everitt, who could "look after themselves".

"It is fair to say that Northampton were like the Wimbledon of the "Crazy Gang days". No one wanted Northampton in the top division and everyone not involved with the club wanted them out. Northampton's case, they got their wish.

"I don't think Joe Broadfoot was there long enough for the other players to form an opinion of him. He came in November and never played after March, Joey played for just five months.

"The problem was it was reported that Joe Broadfoot joined the club for a record transfer fee of £27,000. Sometimes this can be a millstone around the player's neck and supporters expect this type of player to be a "Superman".

"I believe all the players in the Northampton team of 1965-66 were good enough for Division One football. My only question mark was over Bryan Harvey. The Northampton goalkeeper, after a brilliant season in 1964-65 when he saved six penalties, fell to bits in Division One. He was dropped for a spell, but later returned and was never the same player. All the other players were excellent but, as I mentioned earlier, key players missed part of the season through injury and they did not have adequate cover.

"Dave Bowen had an excellent game plan with two attacking wingers and two ball-playing midfielders and we did score quite a few goals. The trouble was we were shipping them in at the other end at a faster rate.

"I did a quick count on Dave Bowen's transfer dealings between 1959 and 1967. In that time, he signed 5 goalkeepers, 13 defenders and 41 attackers. Dave believed that a forward only had three good games out of four and so swapped the forwards around quite a bit. Maybe he had more faith in Bryan Harvey than I thought, as I can't recall him trying to sign another goalkeeper in the Division One days.

"We also had two excellent left-wingers in Barry Lines and Tommy Robson. Both were so different. Lines was more skilful as he would beat his full-back and take the ball to the byline and cross it. Robson liked to cut inside and have a pop at goal. I was not surprised that Robson was sold, as the club turned down an offer of £30,000 for Lines from Arsenal two seasons earlier. The transfer fee we got from Robson gave us money to buy Graham Moore and George Hudson. I felt it was good business, others may feel differently.

"I can't remember the supporters ever having a go at the manager or the team, as they put up such a fight for survival. The odd fan may have had a moan, but on the whole the fans were behind the team. Also, during the 1960s, the press did not try to pick the team like they do nowadays. Like the fans, the local media got behind Northampton town quite well.

"We can always be wise after the event but the directors must take a lot of the blame for Northampton's relegation. They kept closed shop and others should have been invited on to the board in an effort to create more money for the club. As far as the manager is concerned, I don't think Dave Bowen could have done more to keep the club in the top flight."

Ian Davies, former Evening Telegraph reporter: "Northampton's plight hinged around an injury to Terry Branston just before the season started. He, of all the players, had been an inspiration from Division Four to Division One and his absence played a crucial part in the disappointing season that followed.

"Branston's absence put undue pressure on Bryan Harvey, who played such a part in the promotion season. As a result, his confidence went, particularly when going for high balls. Graham Carr's lack of height made a big difference. Division One centre forwards were quick and skilful. They were ready to take advantage of any mistakes.

"Harvey's deputy Norman Coe was a brave goalkeeper, but he was far too short and unable to dominate the penalty area. The shakiness of the goalkeepers put undue pressure on the

A TALE OF TWO FOOTBALL TOWNS & MILLWALL F.C.

defence. Mike Everitt was very consistent and Northampton's left back. He had been at Highbury and was a quality player. Although he had since calmed down a bit, his off-the-field activities caused more than a little trouble.

"Theo Foley was also troubled by injury, but he had been for about three seasons and how he kept going was incredible. He was a good captain and his presence was always valuable to the team.

"Joe Kiernan was best player in the team. He also played in every match. He was a cultured wonderful passer. If he had a fault, it was that he was too attacking at times, sometimes left caught out of position with disastrous results. But over the season, there was little doubt that he was Northampton's best player.

"John Mackin, Vic Cockcroft and Carr were not up to Division One standard. They would have been consistently good in the lower leagues, but they, above all others, exemplified the gap between Division One and the lower divisions.

"Similarly, John Kurilla, Bobby Hunt and Charlie Livesey, I would also have rated as good lower-division players. Hunt scored some good goals, but on the ball he was a liability. And Livesey had been tried and found wanting at both Southampton and Chelsea.

"Graham Moore was a totally different case. Here was a really brilliant footballer. Capped by Wales at the age of 18, Moore was described by Denis Law is the best passer of the ball he had ever seen. Graham's problem was his inability to control powerful frame. As befits a miner, he was partial to several drops of the amber liquid and once had to wear a special plastic suit in training, having come back about three stone overweight.

"Derek Leck was an ex-Millwall player. He was an interesting case. Originally, he was signed as a centre forward. Dave Bowen converted him into a wing half, where he improved out of recognition. During the Division Two promotion season, I would rate him as most consistent player. Like for many of the others, Division One was just out of his reach.

"Bobby Brown was class player, an intelligent man who was a little on the frail site. He scored some wonderful goals and played well when he went to Cardiff.

"George Hudson was another, who was probably the best available 'at the price', but not really a Division One footballer.

"Harry Walden was good Division Three winger, but not in the Joe Broadfoot class.

"Joe Broadfoot was unfortunate to catch the 1966 'no wingers' craze, because he was a real winger. Alf Ramsey won the World Cup without wingers, so all the English managers copied faithfully. Why do we try to make players fit systems? Surely it's better the other way around. Joe was a brilliant player. He had tormented the life out of us at Millwall and Ipswich, and his contribution in Division One was enormous. His exciting runs down the right made him a great crowd pleaser."

A TALE OF TWO FOOTBALL TOWNS & MILLWALL F.C.

Chapter 19: Right. Back to the Den. The summer of 1966.

I was happily driving my cab around London and living there, after the debacle at Northampton Town. I was disappointed they'd got relegated, but I was pleased that Millwall (the first club) had got promoted two years running. Northampton were still paying my wages and I didn't really want to think about my future as a footballer.

At the end of the 1965-66 season, I had done a bit of training down the Den. The Millwall boss Billy Gray had allowed me to. I was so shocked to hear that Billy upped and left Millwall near the end of that season, especially after a successful promotion campaign. Billy left to go back down two divisions with Brentford, who were about to be relegated to Division Four. I've heard since that he had a row with one of the directors but, at the time, I thought he might have fallen out with the chairman, Mickey Purser.

Millwall appointed former Lion Benny Fenton as their new boss. He had been out of the game for a little while, but had managed Orient and before that Colchester United, so he had loads of experience. Anyway, shortly before the season was about to start, I got asked to go and talk to him, and this is what he had to say: "Look, I want you to sign for me. Here you are, number 7." With that, he gave me a circular tag from a hook which had the number 7 on it. "That's your number," he said. But then he added: "I don't want you to play as a winger. Not to begin with, anyway. We need to consolidate in this division first. Then you can move back to the right wing. I promise." It was safety first. I could understand why Benny would want me to play that way at the start of the season, as Millwall might find the second tier of English football a lot more difficult than the third.

Also, playing without wingers was in vogue at the time. England had just won the World Cup without wingers, so now Millwall were about try to succeed by playing the same sort of game.

I was chuffed that Millwall wanted me back because that suited me fine. I'd never been really unhappy during my first stint at Millwall. The only thing that had unsettled me had been the lack of success and the lack of a vision for the future of the club. The crowd had always been great to me down there, so I said: "Yeah, okay."

Millwall gave £1,000 as a signing-on fee, which was a lot of money in those days. And the chairman Mickey Purser kindly gave me a couple of cars. They were one-year old Minis, which were quite valuable. That was very helpful, as I was involved in a car sales business in London.

I was really looking forward to the start of the season, although I knew I wouldn't be playing on the wing.

Funnily enough, one of our first games of the season was a League Cup match against Brentford, now managed by Billy Gray. They beat us over two legs and we didn't score a goal. I was running about trying to do what I was supposed to do. I didn't feel I achieved much, despite all my efforts.

A TALE OF TWO FOOTBALL TOWNS & MILLWALL F.C.

Before that, we'd played Rotherham United away from home in the league, and I'd scored. But we still lost 3-1.

We kept at it though and I did too. I remember scoring the only goal of the game near the end of the game against Coventry at the Den. It was a free kick, so I won't forget that in a hurry!

I also won't forget being called a "C-U-Next-Thursday" (that's swearing, just in case you don't know!) by Eddie Spearrit of Ipswich, as we beat them by the same scoreline. Eddie swore at me right in my ear hole, as he chopped me to the ground. So I went up to him and whacked him in the belly. The crowd started counting him out like he was a boxer. They counted up to ten and Eddie stayed down. The Millwall fans loved it.

In those days, the match official were petrified when they came to the Den. They didn't want to do anything, so I got away with it.

My former Ipswich team-mates weren't too happy with me, but I don't call people names and I didn't expect them to call me names. It was just a reaction.

That result against Ipswich moved us up to 10th in the league, so we were doing really well. By not losing, we'd equaled Reading's record of going 55 home games unbeaten, which had been set back in 1935.

Billy Gray was manager when Millwall first embarked on that remarkable run. Alex Stepney had been in goal then, but had since been sold to Chelsea for £50,000. But other key members of that team were still around when I returned to the club.

In our next game, we almost lost to Carlisle. It was a dismal day and the Den was dead flat for once, in terms of atmosphere. All of a sudden, Carlisle scored. Well, that roused the natives. And cor! The noise they made! They cheered us and roared us on and we equalised. And they went mad. We ended up winning 2-1, with Len Julians scoring both goals, and now the record was ours alone. We'd gone 56 games unbeaten at the Den.

It was a time for celebration. I remember Millwall taking all the players to the Hilton Hotel for a boxing competition. Peter Aliss, the famous golfer, joined us, as did a few other star names.

That kind of thing was enjoyable, but deep down I worried about whether I'd been doing myself justice playing in midfield. I'd scored a few goals and I was doing what Benny Fenton wanted me to do for the team, but it was unnatural for me to play this way. Benny had said I'd only have to play in midfield until we consolidated, but it already looked like we'd done that. I'd agreed to that, although I didn't really know what I was doing. All I wanted to do was come back to Millwall and play in the team. But I wasn't playing at my best. Let's put it that way.

I was playing for the team, I felt, and sacrificing my natural game. So I was bound to make more mistakes than I normally would. Yet, I was chipping in with goals. The goal I scored at

A TALE OF TWO FOOTBALL TOWNS & MILLWALL F.C.

Portsmouth was interesting as it was from a Len Julians knock-down, just before half-time from a corner.

So we went in the dressing room for our team talk at the interval and one of my team-mates was moaning about me hitting a bad pass. I was never the greatest passer of a ball, but Eamonn Dunphy was fuming about it. He came over to me shouting: "What are you trying to do? Get my leg broke?"

Dunphy was swearing, shouting and hollering. He kept on and on at me, so in the end I jumped up and said: "Shut up or I'll f**king flatten you!"

The other players pulled us apart. But I couldn't believe I'd been accused of trying to get one of my team-mates injured. What kind of player would do that? None that I've ever met. Also, I've never met a player who's not played at least one bad pass in his career.

Anyway, we'd beaten Reading's record and, by 14th January 1967, we needed to avoid defeat against Plymouth Argyle to make it 60 games unbeaten at the Den. The Pilgrims weren't expected to put up much of a fight. They were lousy away from home. They hadn't won on their travels in the league that season. We were 3rd and they were 14th in the table.

But we didn't just have Plymouth on our minds. We'd just drawn Tottenham in the FA Cup, so a lot of us were looking forward to playing against them. No wonder there's that old adage in football: "Take one game at a time."

While we were thinking of Spurs, Plymouth were concentrating on the matter at hand. At half-time, we were 2-0 down. They'd capitalised on a weakly-struck Tommy Wilson back pass for one of their goals, I remember that.

It looked the end of the road for our unbeaten record. It was the first time we'd been 2-0 down at home since my return.

The manager, Benny Fenton, must have thought he needed to do something drastic as he called me and Micky Brown over. He said: "I want one of you two to go down injured." That was the only way you could bring on a substitute in those days. It wasn't supposed to be a tactical move at all.

Well, I had gone down injured or exhausted or call it what you like at Northampton's County Ground. The crowd had been chanting: "Broadfoot, Ha! Ha! Ha!' But I silenced them with an early goal. I'd scored a rare header and we'd won 2-1. I even poked my head around their dressing room door after the game and said to my old team-mates: "You must be struggling, if I can score a header against you." They looked back at me in silence. My old team were bottom of the league now.

Anyway, the reason I didn't mind going down in that game was Northampton were trying to kick me off the park. I thought: "I'm not having this," so I stayed down after I'd been fouled. That was after about an hour and George Jacks came on to replace me.

Benny Fenton was asking me to do the same again, when all I wanted to do was preserve Millwall's unbeaten home record.

A TALE OF TWO FOOTBALL TOWNS & MILLWALL F.C.

Micky Brown wasn't having it either. He said to Benny: "Not me, boss. I'm running my f**king b*ll*cks off!" I didn't say anything.

When we kicked off the second half, I decided I'd move out wider to the right like a traditional right winger and we pulled a goal back through Billy Neil. It looked like we might get an equaliser soon.

But then a message reached me from the bench. I was being told to go down injured. I ignored it.

So Benny gave up trying to get me to do it and Micky Brown was to go down instead. Doug Baker replaced him and we ended up losing 2-1. Our 59-game unbeaten run at the Den had come to an end.

And so had my career at Millwall, as I found out on the following Monday. Benny Fenton told me to come to his office. Once I got in there, he said to me: "You're never going to play for me again."

I could have mentioned that was illegal to fake injury. I could have mentioned that he'd never given me a chance to play on the wing. But I just let it go. I said: "Okay, fair enough." And I walked away.

Next thing I knew, I was playing in the reserves against Leyton Orient. I scored a hat-trick from the right wing, so I thought I'd go and ask Benny if he'd give me another chance to play in my best position.

It was about February, by now. But I'd made a big mistake. I'd written a letter to the chairman, Mickey Purser. It said something like: "I'm ever so sorry. I feel I should have been given a chance to play on the right wing. I was only supposed to play in midfield on temporary basis until we consolidated our place in this league, so I'd be grateful if I could have the chance to play in the position where I feel I can serve the club I love best." Or words to that effect.

Obviously, Mickey Purser had to say something to the manager about the letter and now Benny was livid. And he was really rude.

So this time, I said: "Are you going to give me a chance to play on the right wing, like you promised?"

Benny replied: "You're finished as a winger."

In January, I was "finished at Millwall", but a month later I was "finished as a winger" too!

The Benny added: "And you're finished at this club."

I didn't say anything. I just walked out.

I didn't go back to training. I just drove my cab and Millwall continued to pay my wages.

Two weeks later, I got a phone call. I'll tell you all about it in the next chapter.

A TALE OF TWO FOOTBALL TOWNS & MILLWALL F.C.

Chapter 20: It's February 1967. I've been told by my boss Benny Fenton that I'm finished at Millwall. I've also been told I'm finished as a winger. So I'm driving my cab and doing my best to forget about the game.

Millwall were 6th in the table after that rare home defeat against Plymouth, which was my last game. Now in February, they've slipped down to 7th. And I have no future as a footballer.

I'm moping at home. Then the phone rings. I get the message. My career could be back on track. I'm to go up to Ipswich Town FC for talks. I couldn't believe my luck!

I went flying back up the A12 to Ipswich. Bill McGarry was still the manager and he said: "Look, I'm prepared to give you a go, but you've got to move up here and live up here."

I thought: "I'm nearly 27-years-old now. I've got to give it a shot."

Previously, under McGarry, I'd played the best football I'd ever played, so I wanted another shot at that. I couldn't wait. However, I had to move the family up there. They were settled in East Dulwich, London, but now my son, Joe, would have to go to school in Ipswich. He hadn't started primary school yet, so it wouldn't be a major upheaval for him.

Anyway, it was great to be back at Portman Road, and I think I played quite well. When I got there, Ipswich were 10th, three places behind Millwall. By the end of the season, Ipswich were 5th and Millwall were three places behind us!

I remember playing against Millwall for Ipswich on Grand National Day at Portman Road. I was really geed up for it. I thought: "I'll show you if I'm finished as a winger, Benny Fenton!"

After about 5 minutes, I went flying down the wing with the ball and suddenly I had no legs. Harry Cripps had taken them away. I jumped up and we went chest to chest. He was my mate, Harry, but it was a bad tackle. Nowadays, we'd have both got booked or sent off. Back then, you could get away with that sort of foul and that sort of reaction. So we both went unpunished.

Anyway, when I got the ball later on, I just knocked it past Harry and made sure I didn't go near him. I knew Harry was slow. That was his limitation but, on the bumpy pitch at the Den, wingers would struggle to get past him. But I murdered him at Portman Road.

We won 4-1 and I scored. As you can imagine, I was really pleased. After the game, I bumped into the Millwall skipper Brian Snowdon and he said: "Why didn't you play like that for us?"

I was flabbergasted. It seemed as if Benny hadn't told any of the other players what had been going on. I had been playing out of position for Millwall and none of my team-mates had noticed.

I'd really wanted to pay back the fans at Millwall for all they'd done for me, but I felt I couldn't do that playing in midfield. They were terrific to me and I'm sure I could have done more

A TALE OF TWO FOOTBALL TOWNS & MILLWALL F.C.

for them and the team had I been allowed to play on the right wing. And now, here was the Millwall captain seemingly endorsing my opinion. Unknowingly though. It made me wonder if the fans had been similarly hoodwinked.

I owed the Millwall fans so much. Their cheers had given me an extra half a yard of pace. Even on that bobbly old pitch! I just wish I could have repaid them more than I did. I'd scored 6 goals and helped the team consolidate in Division Two, but I wanted to do much more than that. It wasn't enough.

Anyway, I was at Ipswich now and I was buzzing again. It wasn't going to last though. At the end of the 1966-67 season, we went on tour to Belgium and I got an Achilles heel problem. I didn't get anything done about it and it got worse. It was getting really painful.

In the summer, I went swimming in the sea and I thought the problem would go away. It didn't.

During the pre-season, we had a friendly against Halifax Town. In that game, my Achilles tendon went again. It was worse than ever that time. Thereafter, the pain came and went as it pleased!

I remember even before that on our pre-season tour of Scotland, we were playing St Johnstone and they wanted all of our team to visit a brewery on the day of the game. My heel wasn't right, so I didn't want to go. I stayed in bed.

So our boss, Bill McGarry, came up to my room and said: "C'mon, get up. We're going to the brewery."

I said: "I don't want to go, boss. My heel hurts."

So McGarry rested me for that game that night and I was substitute. After about 20 minutes, Danny Hegan (who was in my place) hit his head on the ground. He was a bit concussed, so he had to come off.

So I went on. I played on the right wing and did quite well. I remember hitting the post and the ball coming back to Frank Brogan, who whacked it in. We were 3-0 up against a Scottish First Division side. We'd already beaten Motherwell (another top flight team) 4-0, so I wasn't surprised. But the left back I was up against didn't take too kindly to being taken apart by a second-tier English team. He was giving me loads of verbal. He kept on and kept on.

I didn't hit him, but I had a kick at him. It was a late tackle. And for once a match official did something about it and I got sent off. That didn't do me a lot of good as I was suspended for two weeks by the Scottish FA, who passed their decision on to the English FA, and I had to miss the start of the following season.

Anyway, because of my Achilles heel problem, I wasn't fully fit, so it wasn't a massive blow to be banned. Ipswich started the season pretty well without me and sent me to see a specialist to fix my injury problem. I was knocked out by the general anesthetic, and then the medical team did what we used to call a "manipulation". I don't know what they did, but they cured it. It's never troubled me since!

A TALE OF TWO FOOTBALL TOWNS & MILLWALL F.C.

I was buzzing again on the training ground. I was full of life and Bill McGarry noticed. He asked me: "Are you fit to play on Saturday?"

And like a fool, I replied: "Yes."

We were playing a local "derby" against Norwich City on Saturday 23rd September 1967. We were 5th and they were 14th. We drew 0-0, but we could have won. Unfortunately, I took a corner and the ball came out to Mick McNeil. He smashed it into the net, but I was given offside, so the "goal" was ruled out. I wasn't interfering with play, but the rules were different then.

Anyway, McGarry wasn't happy with me and I got dropped. The team kept winning in the league and drawing sometimes, so I couldn't get back in the team. I had a moan and spoke to the boss. But McGarry said: "I'm paying you first-team money, aren't I? What are you moaning about?"

I said: "I don't want your first-team money. I want to be in the first team."

So Bill McGarry stopped paying me first-team money. I should have kept my mouth shut!

As much as I wanted first-team football, it wasn't too bad playing in the reserves at Ipswich. I was playing alongside a couple of players who would end up as England internationals: Mick Mills and Colin Viljoen. Gerry Baker had also been dropped from the first team, so our reserves were pretty strong.

I wasn't happy though. I'd hardly ever played in the reserves before and didn't feel like starting now. However, I was made captain and I did my best. I remember just before our game against Arsenal reserves, I said to my team-mates: "All for one and one for all!" It was proper "Three Musketeers" stuff!

Anyway, Viljoen, Millsy and I had been working on a free kick in training. I would run over the ball, run past the wall, Millsy would knock it to Viljoen, who would put it behind the wall, and I would crack it in the net.

So against Arsenal reserves, we got a free kick. Millsy knocked it to Viljoen. He put it behind the wall. And just as I was about to strike it into the net past Bob Wilson in the Arsenal goal, I noticed Steve Burtenshaw, their coach, bearing down on me. I thought: "If I'm going to kick this ball, he's going to kick my leg and maybe do a lot of damage." But being captain and feeling brave made a difference. I whacked the ball in and Burtenshaw caught me on my left knee. I was in agony.

Anyway, I was out injured after that. To make matters worse, McGarry said: "I would have put you back in the first team if you'd stayed fit."

He'd said virtually the same when I was suspended, earlier that season: "I would have played you if you weren't banned."

I think McGarry was just trying to keep my spirits up. This injury to my left knee was going to take a long while to get over, that was for sure.

A TALE OF TWO FOOTBALL TOWNS & MILLWALL F.C.

When I did get over it, I remember playing at Leicester City for the reserves. We won and I remember slipping in the mud. My left leg locked. It was only for a moment, but it was a sign of things to come. It started happening more regularly. That kick I'd got at Arsenal had done lasting damage.

It was worrying me, so I got a specialist to look at it. He started feeling my right knee as well. He said: "You've got a cyst on your right knee."

I said: "That's always been there."

He replied: "Well, it's got to come out."

So the specialist decided to give me a double operation on both knees.

After the operation the specialist came to see me and told me my football career was over. He said: "You have knees like a man of 90."

So that was it. Ipswich paid up my wages until the end of the season. I'd already played my last professional game of football against Huddersfield on 20th January 1968. At least, I'd signed off with a win at Portman Road.

But I didn't go straight back down to London. I'd go down there to drive my cab, but I stayed with my family up in Ipswich until October 1968. I was enjoying my golf and winning some money from gambling on it. But then I got kicked out of my local golf club when they found out I'd been betting on myself. I was one of those people you either loved or loathed!

Looking back on my time as a professional footballer, I'd had a good ten years in the game. I was disappointed that I couldn't play on for another five or six years at second or third division level. I was disappointed that I didn't score 100 league goals; I scored 85, so I was only two average seasons away from doing that. Not a bad goal tally for a winger though.

I played 369 league games, which was a lot more than poor old Barry Bell, who twisted his kneecap right round making his league debut for Millwall. His football career lasted only a matter of about 20 minutes because of that horrific injury. So I have to count my blessings.

Although I feel I would have done better had I been coached, I was basically a lazy player. I always did what was easiest. I relied on my speed. I just kicked the ball past a defender and ran. I did practise my left foot a lot and consequently scored a lot of goals with it.

I must have done something right because Harry Redknapp (who was manager of Southampton at the time) came up to me at Millwall, when he saw me in the press area and said: "I remember when you used to fly up the wing. Can you still run that fast?"

I said: "Nah, Harry. I can't run anymore. But I can play golf. I can hit it straight down the middle. Do you fancy a game?"

A TALE OF TWO FOOTBALL TOWNS & MILLWALL F.C.

Harry laughed, but then he had to answer his phone and off he went, wheeling and dealing on the transfer front, no doubt.

Anyway, once I finished playing, I started coaching my old school: Roan. We entered the English Schools' Championship for the first time and we won it. The boys played the way I asked them to, so all credit to them for winning the trophy.

Then I joined the Old Boy's club at Roan and played football for them as a player/manager. I played centre forward and tried to pull the strings from that position. I trained them twice a week and, like the schoolboys, they did as they were told. That made us hard to beat. They all used to get behind the ball, but not many amateur teams did that in those days. Anyway, I had another 10 years playing football for them and, overall, I enjoyed that time.

It helped me get over not playing professional football anymore. But golf helped me even more. I used to drive my cab in London on Friday night and for the weekend. That would earn me enough money, so I could play golf all week. I got down to a 6 handicap but, had I started playing earlier in life, I think I could have been much better at it.

I was also a middle-order batsman and got over 100 fifties for Old Roan. That helped me keep my mind off professional football too.

Unfortunately, my other sporting exploits didn't prevent me getting into trouble from time to time. But maybe that's a story best left for another time.

JOE BROADFOOT

JOE BROADFOOT'S CAREER STATISTICS

Millwall - 1958-63: 225 league appearances - 60 goals

Ipswich - 1963-65: 81 league appearance - 17 goals

Northampton - 1965-66: 17 league appearances - 1 goal

Millwall - 1966-67: 26 appearances - 5 goals

Ipswich - 1967-68: 20 appearances - 2 goals

A TALE OF TWO FOOTBALL TOWNS & MILLWALL F.C.

SEASON BY SEASON

MILLWALL (FIRST STINT)

1958-59: 44 games - 7 goals + 3 FA Cup games & 4 Southern Floodlight Cup games - 1 goal

1959-60: 42 games - 14 goals + 1 FA Cup game & 1 Southern Floodlight Cup game

1960-61: 40 games - 13 goals + 1 League Cup game & 1 Kent FA Challenge Cup final

1961-62: 42 games - 8 goals + 1 FA Cup, 1 League Cup game & 1 Kent FA Challenge Cup final

1962-63: 45 games - 17 goals + 2 FA Cup & 1 League Cup games

1963-64: 12 games - 1 goal + 2 League Cup games

IPSWICH TOWN (FIRST STINT)

1963-64: 29 games - 4 goals + 3 FA Cup games - 1 goal

1964-65: 36 games - 12 goals + 2 FA Cup games & 1 League Cup game

1965-66: 16 games - 1 goal + 4 League Cup games - 1 goal

NORTHAMPTON TOWN

1965-66: 17 games - 1 goal + 1 FA Cup game

MILLWALL (SECOND STINT)

1966-67: 26 games - 5 goals + 2 League Cup games

IPSWICH TOWN (SECOND STINT)

1966-67: 15 games - 2 goals + 3 FA Cup games

1967-68: 5 games + 1 League Cup game

ABOUT JOE BROADFOOT SENIOR

Playing with distinction on the right wing, Joe Broadfoot Sr played in all four professional divisions in England between 1958 and 1968. Joe had two stints with Millwall, two spells with Ipswich Town and a brief 'flirtation' with Northampton Town in their one and only season in the top flight.

ABOUT THE AUTHOR

Joe Broadfoot Jr is a soccer journalist, who also writes fiction and literary criticism. His former experiences as a DJ took him to far-flung places such as Tokyo, Kobe, Beijing, Hong Kong, Jakarta, Cairo, Dubai, Cannes, Oslo, Bergen and Bodo. He is now a CELTA-qualified English teacher with a first-class honours degree in Literature and an MA in Victorian Studies.

A TALE OF TWO FOOTBALL TOWNS & MILLWALL F.C.

JOE BROADFOOT

A TALE OF TWO FOOTBALL TOWNS & MILLWALL F.C.

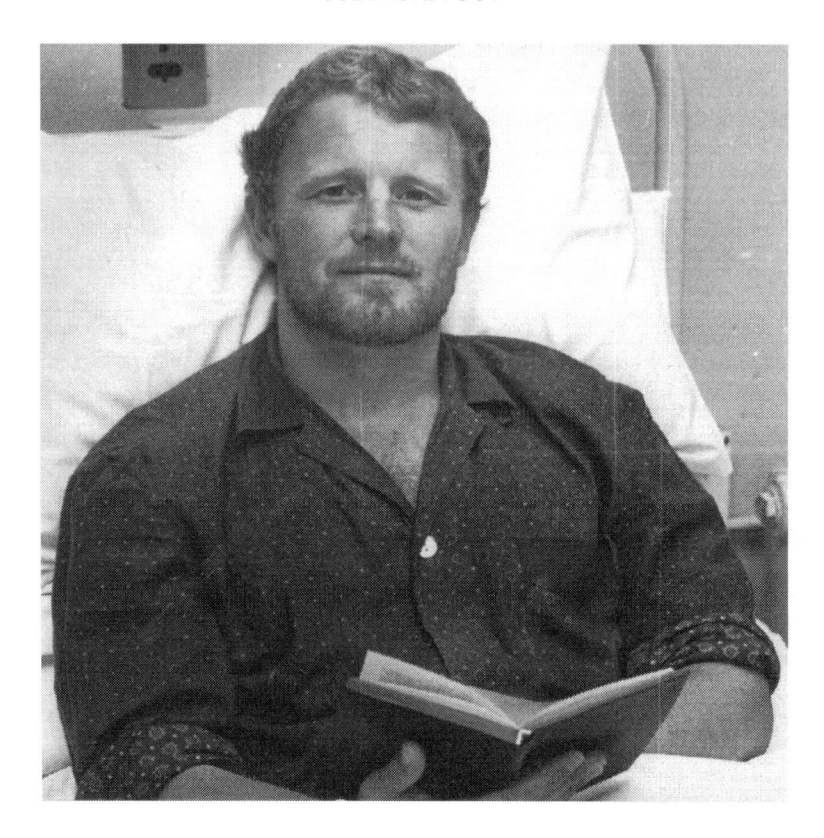

JOE BROADFOOT

Printed in Great Britain
by Amazon